Thomas A. O'Donoghue

Upholding the Faith

The Process of Education in Catholic Schools in Australia, 1922–1965

PETER LANG
New York • Washington, D.C./Baltimore • Bern
Frankfurt am Main • Berlin • Brussels • Vienna • Oxford

Library of Congress Cataloging-in-Publication Data

O'Donoghue, T. A. (Tom A.)
Upholding the faith: the process of education in Catholic schools
in Australia, 1922–1965 / Thomas A. O'Donoghue.
p. cm. — (History of schools and schooling; vol. 24)
Includes bibliographical references and index.
1. Catholic Church—Education—Australia—History—20th century.
I. Title. II. History of schools and schooling; v. 24.
LC509 .O36   371.071'2'94—dc21   2001033164
ISBN 0-8204-5653-5
ISSN 1089-0678

Die Deutsche Bibliothek-CIP-Einheitsaufnahme

O'Donoghue, Thomas A.:
Upholding the faith: the process of education in catholic schools
in Australia, 1922–1965 / Thomas A. O'Donoghue.
−New York; Washington, D.C./Baltimore; Bern;
Frankfurt am Main; Berlin; Brussels; Vienna; Oxford: Lang.
(History of schools and schooling; Vol. 24)
ISBN 0-8204-5653-5

Cover design by Dutton & Sherman Design

The paper in this book meets the guidelines for permanence and durability
of the Committee on Production Guidelines for Book Longevity
of the Council of Library Resources.

Printed in the United States of America

UPHOLDING THE FAITH

HISTORY OF SCHOOLS & SCHOOLING

Alan R. Sadovnik and Susan F. Semel
General Editors

Vol. 24

PETER LANG
New York • Washington, D.C./Baltimore • Bern
Frankfurt am Main • Berlin • Brussels • Vienna • Oxford

Dedication

To Margaret, Deirdre and Sinead

Acknowledgements

In writing this book I benefited greatly from the help provided by many people. My colleague, Clive Whitehead, deserves special mention, not least because of his great patience when the original idea for the book was formulating in my mind. A very special word of appreciation is due to other colleagues who supported me in so many ways, particularly Ann Chapman, Susan Kaldor, Marnie O'Neill, Roger Slee and Lesley Vidovich. The valuable advice provided by Tony Potts of La Trobe University, Denis McLaughlin of the Australian Catholic University, and Stephanie Burley of The University of Adelaide is also gratefully acknowledged. Responsibility for viewpoints and errors of fact, however, lies entirely with me.

I am also pleased to record my thanks to The University of Western Australia for once again giving me generous study leave and financial assistance to undertake the necessary archival work. I incurred a particular debt of gratitude to the staff in the Archives of the Roman Catholic Archdiocese of Perth, and especially to the archivist, Sister Frances Stibi. Finally, I wish to thank Mrs. Zan Blair for her patience and skill in preparing the typescript and for regularly bringing my attention to the most important things in life.

Tom O'Donoghue
The Graduate School of Education
The University of Western Australia
April 2001

Table of Contents

Chapter One

Introduction

The Catholic Church (the Church) has long insisted on the right to organize its own schools, staff them with its own appointees and teach distinctively denominational doctrine. Also, it has insisted that, wherever possible, Catholic parents should send their children to Catholic schools. Consequently, throughout the nineteenth century the Church expressed deep opposition to the great increase in state intervention in education internationally and it mounted resistance wherever possible. It fought a losing battle and by the 1920s there was only a small number of countries where it was satisfied with the school system.[1] Australia was not one of these countries.

A British penal colony was established in Australia when Captain Arthur Phillip and his party of soldiers, sailors and convicts landed where Sydney is today. Following the establishment of the original colony of New South Wales, six colonies emerged in total, with the government and administration of each being centralized in the capital cities. While the colonies were very strongly British and Protestant both socially and culturally, they also had a significant Irish Catholic minority.

By the time the transportation of convicts ceased, the white settlers of Australia had developed an expectation that their centralized colonial governments would provide public services. The general pattern by 1850 regarding educational provision was a mixture of governmental enterprise, occasional voluntary effort and state assistance to denominational schools. This situation was brought about through the insistence of the Anglican, Presbyterian and Catholic

Churches that the control of teaching was their responsibility, as education and moral training were inseparable. Their pressure resulted in grants being paid to religious societies to assist in payment of teachers' salaries and the cost of school buildings. Change, however, was on the horizon.

At the time of Federation in 1901 each Australian state had established a system of primary schools providing free, compulsory and secular primary education controlled by government departments.[2] A growth in government preference for non-denominational education between 1872 and 1893 had led to the abolition of financial aid to denominational schools in each colony. Catholic education was particularly badly hit by the associated acts[3] and it was not until the 1950s and 1960s that Catholic schools once again began to benefit from even a small amount of government financial assistance.[4] It was the establishment of the Karmel Committee in 1972, due to the near financial collapse of many Australian Catholic schools because of rising costs, which really turned the tide. The outcome of this development was the adoption of the recommendations of the committee,[5] resulting in the great majority of Catholic schools in particular obtaining approximately 80 per cent of their costs from Australian state or federal governments, and being able to apply for capital grants for refurbishing or extending schools.

Notwithstanding the lack of substantial state aid for nearly one hundred years, the Catholic Church in Australia was successful not only in maintaining, but also in expanding an educational sector independent of state educational systems.[6] Yet the general structure of Catholic schooling since the early 1900s reflected that of the Australian state systems in having a primary school level and a secondary school level as two distinct educational phases. To maintain credibility and facilitate social mobility, Catholic primary schools also adopted the various syllabi prescribed for state schools, with their emphasis on the three-Rs, while Catholic secondary schools came under the domination of state public examinations. Thus, one   is prompted to ask what was distinctive about Catholic education in Australia. One answer to this question centers on the private nature of Catholic education, which resulted in great freedom for the Church at the level of school management and administration. What is important within the present context, however, is that such freedom was sought and maintained, albeit at enormous financial and human expense, so the Church could ensure that the process of education in its schools was to its satisfaction.

The distinctiveness of the process of education in Australian Catholic schools in the past is touched upon tangentially in the excellent studies by Praetz[7] and O'Brien.[8] Fogarty's[9] book, which charts the provision of Catholic education in Australia over the period 1806–1950, is the only work which gives the matter some focused attention by centering on the religious and 'secular' curriculum, as well as on some aspects of 'the hidden curriculum'. While this was a pioneering work when it appeared in 1959, it neglected a variety of issues, including the construction of gender and the fact that certain religious orders favored the teaching of particular social groups rather than others. The book also presupposed a significant amount of cultural and institutional knowledge pertaining to the Catholic Church on the part of the reader. Furthermore, with no comparable book appearing since then, the questions which Musgrave[10] posed in 1979, namely, what happened in the Catholic classroom and how did it differ from what happened in Protestant, Jewish or secular classrooms, have still not been the subject of an extensive treatise.

This book goes some way towards addressing the deficit by focusing on four distinctive features of the process of education in Catholic schools in Australia during the period 1922–65. First, Catholic education was conducted within an authoritarian framework. Secondly, a major emphasis was placed on religious instruction and on ensuring that schooling had a religious atmosphere which was all pervasive. Thirdly, particular gender roles were promoted on the grounds that they constituted those roles best fitted to ensuring the salvation of 'the faithful'. Fourthly, there was a very strong Irish influence in pupils' experience of schooling.

To focus only on the period 1922–65 does not imply that the period prior to this and the periods since then are not worthy of examination. Rather, it is recognized that such an examination would lead to major works in themselves. Also, the period 1922–65 constituted a distinct era in the history of the Catholic Church, not only nationally but internationally. The year 1922 marked the beginning of the reign of Pope Pius XI, the 'social action Pope', who placed great emphasis on Catholics confronting modernism head-on and on attempting to shape society in accordance with Catholic social teaching. The following years witnessed a number of significant developments for Catholic education in Australia. The year 1929 signaled the beginning of the Great Depression, during which Catholic schools in the nation were kept vibrant only through the efforts of the large number of Australian and overseas nuns, religious brothers and priests who both managed and staffed them on very low budgets. Equally significant was the beginning of a reduction in vocations to the religious life from about the middle of the 1950s. Also, as has already been pointed out, by the early 1960s the Commonwealth Government had begun to provide some public funding for non-government schools. Finally, the year 1965 marked the end of the Second Vatican Council (1962–65) and the resulting 'opening up' of the Church internationally. Associated with this 'opening up' were enormous challenges to the 'traditional' Catholic 'mind-set' and religious practices. Thus was ushered in not just a new era in Catholic education in Australia, but a whole new era in Australian Catholicism in general.

The research which led to this book commenced with a variety of questions for the identification of sources required to address the central research question of what was distinctive about the process of education in Catholic schools in Australia during the period 1922–65. The pursuit of these questions suggested a broad range of areas for exploration. For example, recognition that conditions such as "time, space, culture, economic status, [and] technological status"[11] can act either to facilitate or constrain the strategies taken within a specific context by an individual or a group, led to an examination of the physical, economic, social and cultural environments within which teachers in Australia worked during the period 1922–65. Similarly, considering what was distinctive about those who constituted the Catholic teaching force during the period led to an examination of such issues as the geographical, ethnic and social origins of those who entered religious teaching orders, the traditions of these orders, their recruitment practices, their programs for the personal and spiritual formation of their members, their teacher training, and their daily routines. Eventually, the questions which were pursued were categorized into three broad sets, namely, questions regarding what was distinctive about those who taught in Catholic schools in Australia during the period in question, questions regarding what was distinctive about the educational experiences which were presented to students, and questions regarding what was distinctive about the approach to teaching which was adopted. The accounts developed in response to each of these sets of research questions are woven into the exposition presented in the various chapters in this book.

The first set of research questions addressed what was distinctive about those who taught in Catholic schools in Australia during the period in question. This put the focus very much on the 'ordinary' teacher in Catholic schools. In the United States educational historians became particularly active during the 1980s in studying the lives of 'ordinary' teachers,[12] leading Warren[13] to conclude that they made schools and classrooms of the past accessible and gave voice to the reflections and commentary of teachers themselves, "the otherwise 'unremarkable' people who delivered school to the nation's children over the course of two centuries". Research in this vein continued in the United States into the 1990s.[14] As it developed in both quality and extent, however, Silver[15] argued that, apart from similar work in Canada, the remainder of the English-speaking world was not quite as active. More recently, Gardner and Cunningham[16] have drawn attention to the fact that teachers constitute "an occupational group about whom, at least in the British context, we know surprisingly little".

Historians in Australia have been more productive than their British counterparts in this field. Here, the focus has tended to be on particular aspects of teachers' lives. Feminist historians[17] have been major contributors. Associated work has been undertaken on the role that teachers have played historically in the construction of masculinity[18] and femininity.[19] The research of Spaull and colleagues[20] on teaching and teacher unionization is equally significant as it provides essential historical perspectives for understanding the pressures under which teachers worked in the past. Further insights into Australian teachers' lives are provided by a small body of research which has attempted to portray the economic, social and cultural contexts of teachers' everyday working environments[21] and by significant biographical works on influential Australian educationalists, including Catholic educationalists.[22]

There is a need, however, to balance trends to date with more 'holistic' perspectives. Warren,[23] focusing on the U.S. context, took up this point over twelve years ago and highlighted it by attending to the growth in the work of feminist historians. His argument was that while historical research on teachers "owes much of its compelling insight and empirical toughness to current interest in women's history", examining the history of teachers only through a gender-sensitive lens can lead us to miss certain important details. He concluded that historians should be wary about blurring distinctions between women's history and the history of teachers. To this we can add that presenting teachers as just male and female can lead to failure to take other issues into consideration, such as class and race.

These observations are equally significant for the Australian context. Also significant for this context is the need to consider religious differences. Such differences can go beyond those of a denominational nature, as illustrated for the Catholic context by a variety of distinctions within the Church itself, including those drawn between 'choir nuns', 'lay nuns' and 'secular female teachers'.[24] This is not to ignore the work of those feminist historians who have acknowledged nuns as teachers in Australian schools.[25] Rather, the contributions of these historians also highlight the need for a much greater research project in the area. Equally, they serve to remind us that there is hardly any research at all which provides insights into the lives of religious brothers, priests, and Catholic and non-Catholic lay people who taught in Catholic schools. Furthermore, this lacuna is not peculiar to Australian educational historiography; even the extensive corpus of research which had been compiled by the early 1990s on the history of education in the United States and Britain did not add up "to a serious, widespread historical commitment to bringing the parochial school, the Catholic, the Christian, the religious experience into the canon of educational history".[26]

Highlighting the need to study the history of the lives of teachers who taught in Catholic schools in Australia also demonstrates the need to balance those studies which have focused on teacher unionization in the country with studies which consider the extent to which Catholic teachers, and particularly those in religious life, were influenced, not by 'industrial' and 'labor' perspectives on teaching, but rather by discourses of 'vocation' and 'the giving of service'. Analyses should also allow for the overlaps which regularly occurred as teachers' professional lives and their personal lives impinged on each other.[27] Finally, it needs to be kept in mind that the plethora of histories on Catholic educational institutions throughout Australia, while extremely valuable in terms of their primary focus, have largely tended to ignore the lives of the 'ordinary' teachers in Catholic schools, including their pedagogical roles, their work outside classrooms and their general day-to-day activities. This book goes some way towards rectifying the deficit in the literature for the period 1922–65, highlighting in particular the fact that the great majority of teachers in Catholic schools were nuns and that they, like their religious brother and priest colleagues, were predominantly influenced by their 'religious formation' in the approaches they adopted as teachers.

The second set of research questions which underpin the study upon which this book is based focused on what was distinctive about the educational experiences which were presented to students in Catholic schools during the period 1922–65. This set of questions arose out of a recognition that while Catholic schools followed the pattern found in state schools of offering state curricula and preparing for public examinations, there was also specific Catholic content taught, most notably in explicit fashion, as in the case of religious instruction, but also implicitly through the other subjects on the curriculum. It was also recognized that very little is known about the nature and detail of such practices. In this, the situation reflects the history of curriculum in other educational sectors in Australia. In other words, while the 'history of education' in general in Australia is a well-developed field of study on many issues, the history of curriculum has been very much neglected. Significant exceptions in this regard are the works of Marsh,[28] Musgrave[29] and Price.[30]

Some excellent studies of other societies provide useful models and theories for shaping thinking and focusing questioning on the history of curriculum in Australia with regard to Catholic schools, state schools and the schools of other religious denominations. In the area of general curriculum history are works such as those of Finkelstein,[31] Franklin[32] and Kliebard[33] on the history of the American school curriculum, and the work of Tomkins[34] on the history of the Canadian school curriculum. There is also considerable published work on the history of individual school subjects. This includes country-specific studies such as those by McCulloch[35] and McCulloch et al.,[36] as well as those of Goodson,[37] which contain studies pertaining to several societies. These are all very useful in stimulating thinking and raising new perspectives on the situation in Australia, including, in particular, the situation in Australian Catholic schools for the period under investigation.

The position of Goodson is also helpful in providing a theoretical framework for examining both how and why state prescribed curricula were accommodated within Catholic schools in Australia. This position rejects the view of the written curriculum as a neutral given embedded in an otherwise meaningful complex situation. Rather, it proposes a view of the curriculum as a social artifact, conceived of and made for deliberate human purposes. Goodson develops this position in a proposal that curriculum history should be studied at the levels of what he terms the 'preactive curriculum' and the 'interactive curriculum'. To study curriculum history at the 'preactive' level is to focus on the plans or syllabi which outline what was intended to happen in a course or program. It involves studying not only the structures and patterns within such documents, but also identifying the various individuals and interest groups involved in their production, and the nature and extent of their influence. For the present work this meant in particular an examination of the religious education programs prescribed by the Catholic Church authorities in Australia during the period 1922–65, but equally it meant that explicit adaptations of official programs in other subjects through arrangements with state authorities had to be analyzed. The insights provided by schemes devised by Eraut et al.,[38] Gall[39] and Piper[40] proved helpful in this regard.

Goodson[41] also argues that that there is not a direct or easily discernible relationship between the 'preactive' definition of a school subject's programs and syllabi, and its interactive realization in the classrooms. To adopt such a perspective is to argue for a study of the 'interactive curriculum', focusing on how the 'preactive curriculum' was mediated by teachers. This is a particularly important focus to adopt in relation to Catholic teachers in Australia during the period under investigation who, because of the distinct shared worldview into which they were socialized through their religious training, were likely to have mediated the curricula for state examinations in particular ways.[42] At the same time, it must be highlighted that the manner in which the curriculum, the pedagogical practices and the general school climate were received by students was not addressed in the research. This very important area of investigation necessitates a separate major research project. The present work establishes the foundations upon which such a project can be formulated.

The third set of research questions underpinning the study upon which this book is based addressed what was distinctive about the approach to teaching which was adopted in Catholic schools in Australia during the period 1922–65. Addressing such questions requires the adoption of some model of the teaching process because, as Cuban[43] puts it, classrooms are "marked by a bewildering variety of student and teacher behaviors". Cuban also offers a helpful approach with his notion that "a limited but useful set of indicators describing important dimensions of what teachers did in their classrooms" is provided by a concept of teaching "as a continuum stretching from teacher-centered to student-centered".[44] Teacher-centered instruction as Cuban defines it, means that a teacher controls what is taught, when, and under what conditions within his or her classroom. Student-centered instruction, on the other hand, means that students "exercise a substantial degree of direction and responsibility for what is taught, how it is learned, and for any movement within the classroom".[45] In offering a set of observable measures of each form of instruction, Cuban recognizes that while they cannot capture the richness of the classroom, nonetheless, they can be used as "a handy wedge in prying open the closed doors of classrooms that existed decades ago" and can help in "mapping, in a preliminary fashion, their pedagogical terrain".[46]

Cuban's model for approaching the historical study of teaching was very useful in examining what was distinctive about the approach to teaching adopted in Catholic schools in Australia during the period 1922–65. In particular, it provided a framework in which to locate the official pedagogical approaches of some of the religious orders. The best known of these approaches is the Jesuit's Ratio Studiorum, with its emphasis on mental training in logical argument—thesis, evidence, objections, discussion and final proof. Among the other religious orders teaching in Catholic schools in Australia to develop distinctive pedagogical theories and approaches were the Ursuline Sisters and the Marist and De La Salle Brothers. Most of the orders, however, based their approaches on inherited practices which, while they had developed in ad hoc fashion over the years, had, by the period in question, taken on certain distinctive patterns.

The limitations of Cuban's model were also recognized when conducting research for this book. In particular, cognizance was taken of recent calls not to concentrate solely on visible interactions when studying the history of the classroom, but to take into account matters such as school climate.[47] Consideration was also given to ways in which various religious orders adapted their pedagogical traditions to Australian circumstances, to the nature of the teacher training received by their members, and to the extent to which members gave advice and support to each other in their lesson planning, their classroom activities and their assessment practices.

Various sources, both written and oral, were identified and drawn upon. These included the 'rules and constitutions' and 'acts of chapter' of religious orders, school annuals, school yearbooks, and reports on education in Catholic newspapers. The many histories of religious congregations in Australia which have been written, particularly over the last twenty years, were also consulted. These were supplemented by oral sources based on interviews with a wide range of individuals who taught in Catholic schools in Australia between 1922 and 1965. One purpose of these interviews was to unearth descriptive data on which the written evidence is silent,[48] as well as to extend and enrich that which is available. The main focus, however, was to construct the 'life stories'[49] of the teachers and develop an understanding of the 'perspectives' they held regarding what it meant to be a teacher in Catholic schools at the time they were teaching and how they acted in light of these perspectives.[50] Silver went some way towards arguing for such an approach in studying the lives of teachers when he argued for "the history of opinion", which he defined as "the history of how people, groups of people, people in action, have interpreted and reinterpreted their world".[51] Such an approach is now reflected in contemporary trends in the writing of educational biography.[52]

This book is based on a synthesis of the results of the research approach outlined so far. It is a general exposition rather than one providing detailed accounts of specific schools and dealing with the many exceptions to the broad features outlined. It is organized into seven chapters. Following this Introduction, chapter 2 commences by highlighting the large amount of cheap labor provided in Catholic schools in Australia by teachers who were members of religious orders. So great was this provision that Catholic education from 1922 to 1965 was dominated by those in religious life. Two major patterns within this dominance need to be considered in providing a broad background to an examination of what was distinctive about the process of education in Catholic schools in Australia during the period. First, while the teaching force was made up almost entirely of nuns, religious brothers and priests, the number of nuns greatly exceeded that of their male colleagues. Secondly, the various religious orders which ran the Catholic schools operated largely independent of each other. Thus, no major structure existed throughout the period for the systematic long-term planning which would have been required to build a coordinated Catholic education system and ensure the economical application of resources.

Chapter 3 is an exposition on the first of the four major features identified in response to the central question of what was distinctive about the process of education in Catholic schools in Australia between 1922 and 1965. The major emphasis of this exposition is on the authoritarian framework which underpinned the preparation programs of those who joined religious orders so that they might live a life based on an observance of the vows of poverty, chastity and obedience, the overiding goal being the attainment of perfection by union with God. The chapter then considers how the teacher training received by those who were members of Catholic religious orders was in the same mould. It also demonstrates that the authoritarian framework extended to the conduct of Catholic schools, thus ensuring that the habitual ways in which a member of a religious order was trained to think and act were not threatened when he or she commenced work as a regular teacher.

Chapter 4 extends the exposition presented in the previous chapter by considering the emphasis placed on religion in the schools. The nature and extent of this emphasis resulted from the major expectation of the Catholic Church in Australia, as elsewhere, that its schools would play a central part in creating within students a belief in, and adherence to, its teachings. It was an emphasis which manifested itself in three major ways: through the formal teaching of religion classes, through the manner in which the teaching of 'secular' subjects was impregnated with religious content, and through a range of practices which ensured production of an all-pervasive religious atmosphere.

Chapter 5 builds on the central position underpinning chapter 4, namely, that the overall aim of Catholic education, regardless of the country concerned, has always been the preparation of students for a fuller life in eternity. During the period under consideration, such preparation was interpreted largely to mean receiving instruction in religious dogma and following the Church's rules. Against such a background, however, the Church in Australia also emphasized particular gender roles on the grounds that they constituted those roles best fitted to ensuring the salvation of the faithful. The part played by the Catholic schools in responding to this emphasis is considered. In particular, it is argued that the construction of gender in Catholic schools has to be viewed primarily as having been influenced by religious considerations. The situation differed sharply from that in state schools and schools run by other religious denominations since pupils in Catholic schools were regularly reminded that the almost asexual state of being a priest, religious brother or nun was the highest state one could achieve within the Church's hierarchy of vocations. Furthermore, while the personal qualities emphasized for the remainder of the Catholic population matched Australian stereotypes in a variety of ways, what gave them their distinctive mark was that they were justified on religious grounds.

In chapter 6 it is argued that while the Catholic Church in Australia became more diverse with each passing year during the period 1922–65, a very strong Irish influence continued to prevail. First, the correspondence between Australian Catholicism and Irish Catholicism is treated briefly, the argument being that it was Irish Catholicism which continued to dominate in the Australian schools. The chapter then goes on to consider how, despite their declining numbers, Irish nuns, religious brothers and priests continued to have a significant presence in the schools, thus playing a major part in perpetuating Irish Catholicism amongst future generations. Finally, attention is paid to the extent to which these same Irish nuns, religious brothers and priests also helped to perpetuate a notion that it was Ireland rather than Britain which constituted 'the mother country' for Australian Catholics.

Chapter 7 returns to the general context. Here it is argued that much of the Catholic Church's effort in education in Australia by the end of the nineteenth century and the beginning of the twentieth century was part of its wider scheme of breaking down the link between being Catholic and being working class. The Church's policy was aimed at elevating the status of Catholics in Australian society so that the status of the Church itself would, in turn, be elevated. In this way, it sought to overcome the Protestant ascendancy's practices aimed at keeping Catholics in a subordinate position. Steadily, Australian Catholics moved up the social ladder. Nevertheless, their sense of suspicion, bitterness and resentment lived on throughout the first half of the twentieth century. This was reinforced by the feeling of injustice at being deprived of financial assistance for their schools and the continuing sectarianism they experienced in the workplace. Concerned with maintaining their improved social position and with moving more assertively into the wider society, they responded with a new confidence. A major contributor to the development of this confidence was the process of education. The Church's schools gave Catholics in Australia a sense of purpose and a sense of identity of which they could be proud.

Overall, this book is offered as a contribution to the development of a new and specialized account for the Australian context of schools as workplaces "which constitute the arena of educational action, where curricula, pedagogies, and policies can be seen as dynamic processes shaped not only by teachers' professional concerns"[53], but also by their lives in general. Along with filling a void in the literature on the social history of teaching in Catholic schools in Australia and elsewhere for the period in question, it is a study which opens up the field for similar studies on other periods and on teachers in state educational sectors, as well as on teachers in schools of other religious denominations. It also lays the groundwork for related studies, focusing specifically on the views of the major stakeholders, including parents and students. Finally, it should be insightful for policy makers by contributing to an understanding of how, over the greater course of time, Catholic teachers have responded to innovation and change. This perspective of decades of collective practice provided by the book constitutes a major resource through which to reflect critically on the existing knowledge base on teachers' careers,[54] teachers' professional lives[55] and teachers' life cycles.[56]

Notes

[1] See J. Whyte, *Church and State in Modern Ireland* (Dublin: Gill and Macmillan, 1971), p. 16.

[2] See D. White, *Education and the State: Federal Involvement in Educational Policy Development* (Victoria, Australia: Deakin University Press, 1987).

[3] Ibid., p. 7.

[4] Ibid., pp. 15–20.

[5] See Australian Schools Commission (Report of the Interim Committee for the Australian Schools Commission, P. Karmel, Chairman), *Schools in Australia* (Canberra, Australia: Australian Government Printing Service, 1973).

[6] The Church never gave up its agitation for state aid. This has led to an abundance of hagiographic literature on individual schools, and on individual orders and their leaders. For an outline of a number of titles of such works see A. Cooper, 'A select bibliography', *The Australasian Catholic Record*, Vol. 25, No. 2, 1998, pp. 164–179. These works reflect the preoccupation of 'mainline'

historians of the Church with documenting the activities of clerical decision-makers and the physical expansion of structures. For a discussion on this see K. Massam, *Sacred Threads: Catholic Spirituality in Australia 1922–1962* (Sydney: University of New South Wales Press, 1996), p. 3. See also J. D. Bollen, A. E. Cahill, B. Mansfield and P. O' Farrell, 'Australian religious history 1960–80', *Journal of Religious History*, Vol. 11, 1980, pp. 8–44.

While the existing body of historical work is instructive, a wide variety of issues remains to be investigated in depth. Much more research needs to be undertaken on the history of Catholic teacher training. Some inroads have been made in B. J. Duncan, 'An analysis of the primary teacher education of the Sisters of Mercy, the Christian Brothers and their lay teachers in Queensland from 1859 to 1979' (unpublished Ph.D. thesis, The University of Queensland, 1984). One of the few works to investigate the manner in which Catholic lay teachers in the schools were kept out of policy making until the 1970s is R. W. Bennett, 'Changes in the Catholic school system in the Maitland Diocese resulting from an increased proportion of lay teachers staffing these schools' (unpublished M.Ed. thesis, University of Newcastle, 1978). Very little work has been undertaken on the adaptation of European religious teaching orders to Australian conditions. An exception is W. A. Greening, 'The adaptation of the Irish Christian Brothers' education system to Australian conditions in the nineteenth century' (unpublished Ph.D. thesis, The University of Melbourne, 1989). The resistance of Catholic women in religious orders to the patriarchal structure of the Church is only beginning to be addressed. See C. N. Lewis, 'Provision for the education of Catholic women in Australia since 1840' (unpublished Ph.D. thesis, The University of Melbourne, 1990); M. R. MacGinley, *A Dynamic of Hope: Institutes of Women Religious in Australia* (Sydney: Crossing Press, 1996); M. M. McKenzie, 'Catholic religious women educators as agents of social change' (unpublished M.A. thesis, Monash University, 1994). Similarly, it is only recently that critical analyses have been undertaken of the work of Catholic orphanages. See, for example, M. S. McGrath, *These Women? Women Religious in the History of Australia. The Sisters of Mercy at Parramatta 1888–1988* (Sydney: The Sisters of Mercy, 1991); B. M. Coldrey, *Child Migration and the Western Australian Boys' Homes* (Victoria, Australia: Tamanaraik Publishing, 1991).

Studies of 'the lived experience' of teachers and pupils in Catholic schools are very much in their infancy (see, for example, C. Trimingham-Jack, 'The lay sister in educational history and memory', Proceedings of the ANZHES Annual Conference, Auckland, 1998). Again, this reflects the situation regarding the general history of Catholicism in Australia; to date the only major historical exploration of the possibilities which the signs and symbols of the institutional Church articulated to the Catholic people of Australia is that undertaken by Massam for the period 1922–62 (see K. Massam, *Sacred Threads: Catholic Spirituality in Australia 1922–1962*). Also, very little is known about the internal politics and tensions within and between the religious orders, including those involved in education, although anecdotal evidence suggests that this is a very fruitful avenue for research.

[7] H. Praetz, *Building a School System: A Sociological Study of Catholic Education* (Melbourne: Melbourne University Press, 1980).

[8] A. O'Brien, *Blazing a Trail: Catholic Education in Victoria, 1963–1980* (Melbourne: David Lovell Publishing, 1999).

[9] R. Fogarty, *Catholic Education in Australia 1806–1950* (Melbourne: Melbourne University Press, 1959).

[10] See H. Praetz, *Building a School System: A Sociological Study of Catholic Education,* p. x.

[11] A. Strauss and J. Corbin, *Basics of Qualitative Research* (Newbury Park, California: Sage, 1990), p. 103.

[12] See L. Cuban, *How Teachers Taught: Constancy and Change in American Classrooms, 1890–1980* (New York: Longman, 1984). See also B. Finkelstein, *Governing the Young: Teacher Behaviour in Popular Primary Schools in Nineteenth Century United States* (London: The Falmer Press, 1989).

[13] D. Warren, 'Messages from the inside: Teachers as clues in history and policy', *International Journal of Educational Research,* Vol. 13, 1989, pp. 379–390.

[14] See R. J. Altenbaugh (ed.), *The Teacher's Voice* (London: The Falmer Press, 1992); R. J. Altenbaugh, 'Oral history, American teachers and the social history of schooling', *Cambridge Journal of Education,* Vol. 27, No. 3, 1997, pp. 313–330; B. Finkelstein, 'Classroom management in the United States', in N. K. Shimahara (ed.), *Politics of Classroom Life: Classroom Life in International Perspective* (New York: Garland Publishing, Inc., 1998).

[15] H. Silver, 'Historiography of education', in T. Husen and T. N. Postlethwaite, (eds.), *The International Encyclopaedia of Education* (London: Pergamon, 1994), p. 2616.

[16] P. Gardner and P. Cunningham, 'Oral history and teachers' professional practice', *Cambridge Journal of Education,* Vol. 27, No. 3, 1997, p. 331.

[17] See, for example, N. K. Kyle, *Her Natural Destiny* (NSW, Australia: New South Wales University Press, 1986); N. K. Kyle (ed.), *Women as Educators in 19th and 20th Century Australia* (Wollongong, Australia: University of Wollongong, School of Learning Studies, 1989); A. Mackinnon, 'A new point of departure', *History of Education Review,* Vol. 13, No. 2, 1984, pp. 1–4; M. Theobald, *Knowing Women: Origins of Women's Education in 19th Century Australia* (Cambridge: Cambridge University Press, 1996).

[18] I. D. Brice, 'Australian boys' schools and the historical constructions of masculinity', Proceedings of the ANZHES Annual Conference, Sydney, 1995.

[19] M. R. Theobald, 'History of women's education in Australia', in T. Husen and T. N. Postlethwaite (eds.), *The International Encyclopaedia of Education,* pp. 6731–6735.

[20] See A. Spaull (ed.), *Australian Teachers from Schoolmasters to Militant Professionals* (South Melbourne, Australia: Macmillan, 1977); A. Spaull, *A History of Federal Teachers' Unions in Australia, 1921–85* (Canberra, Australia: Australian Teachers' Federation, 1985); A. Spaull and M. Sullivan, *A History of the Queensland Teachers' Union* (Sydney: Allen and Unwin, 1989).

[21] See, for example, R. J. W. Selleck and M. G. Sullivan, (eds.), *Not so Eminent Victorians* (Melbourne: Melbourne University Press, 1982); E. Clarke, *Female*

Teachers in Queensland State Schools: A History 1860–1983 (Brisbane: Department of Education Policy and Information Services Branch, June 1985); O. Ford, 'Voices from below: Family, school and community in the Braybrook Plains 1854–1892' (unpublished M.Ed. thesis, The University of Melbourne, 1993).

22   See A. Cooper, 'A select bibliography', pp. 164–179.

23   See D. Warren, 'Messages from the inside: Teachers as clues in history and policy', *International Journal of Educational Research*, Vol. 13, 1989, p. 386.

24   See S. Burley, 'Lost leaders from the convent and the classroom 1880–1925', in J. McMahon, H. Neidhart and J. Chapman (eds.), *Leading the Catholic School* (Richmond, Victoria Australia: Spectrum, 1997), p. 52.

25   See N. K. Kyle, *Her Natural Destiny*; C. N. Lewis, 'Provision for the education of Catholic women in Australia since 1840' (unpublished Ph.D. thesis, University of Melbourne, 1990); C. Trimingham Jack, 'The lay sister in educational history and memory', Proceedings of the ANZHES Annual Conference, Auckland, New Zealand, 1998.

26   H. Silver, 'Knowing and not knowing in the history of education', *History of Education*, Vol. 21, No. 1, 1992, p. 103.

27   R. J. Altenbaugh, 'Oral history, American teachers and the social history of schooling', p. 324.

28   C. Marsh, 'The development of a senior school geography curriculum in Western Australia 1964–1984', in I. F. Goodson (ed.), *School Subjects and Curriculum Change: Case Studies in the Social History of Curriculum* (Dover, New Hampshire: Croom Helm, 1987), pp. 179–208.

29   P. W. Musgrave, *Society and the Curriculum in Australia* (Sydney: George Allen and Unwin, 1979).

30   M. H. Price, *The Development of the Secondary School Curriculum* (Dover, New Hampshire: Croom Helm, 1986).

31   B. Finkelstein, *Governing the Young: Teacher Behaviour in Popular Primary Schools in Nineteenth Century United States.*

32   B. Franklin, *Building the American Community: The School Curriculum and the Search for Social Control* (Philadelphia: Falmer Press, 1986).

33   H. M. Kliebard, *The Struggle for the American Curriculum, 1893–1958* (Boston: Routledge and Kegan Paul, 1986).

34   G. Tomkins, *A Common Countenance: Stability and Change in the Canadian Curriculum* (Scarborough, Ontario, Canada: Prentice-Hall, 1986).

35   G. McCulloch, *The Secondary Technical School: A Usable Past?* (London: Falmer Press, 1990).

36   G. McCulloch, E. Jenkins and D. Layton, *Technological Revolution? The Politics of School Science and Technology in England and Wales Since 1945* (London: Falmer Press, 1985).

37   See I. F. Goodson, *School Subjects and Curriculum Change: The School Curriculum and the Search for Social Control* (Dover, New Hampshire: Croom Helm, 1983); *Social Histories of the Secondary School Curriculum: Subjects for Study* (Dover, New Hampshire: Croom Helm, 1985); *International Perspectives in Curriculum History* (Dover, New Hampshire: Croom Helm,

1987); *The Making of Curriculum: Collected Essays* (New York: The Falmer Press, 1988); 'Studying school subjects', *Curriculum Perspectives*, Vol. 12, No. 1, 1992, pp. 23–26.

[38] M. Eraut, L. Goad and G. Smith, *The Analysis of Curriculum Materials* (Brighton, England: University of Sussex, 1975).

[39] M. D. Gall, *Handbook for Evaluating and Selecting Curriculum Materials* (Boston: Allyn and Unwin, 1981).

[40] K. Piper, *Evaluation and the Social Sciences* (Canberra, Australia: Australian Government Printing Service, 1976).

[41] See I. F. Goodson, 'Studying school subjects', pp. 23–26.

[42] For an elaboration on this argument see A. R. King and J. A. Brownell, *The Curriculum and the Disciplines of Knowledge* (New York: John Wiley and Sons, 1966), p. 26.

[43] L. Cuban, *How Teachers Taught: Constancy and Change in American Classrooms, 1890–1980*, p. 3.

[44] Ibid.

[45] Ibid.

[46] Ibid.

[47] See K. Dams, M. Depaepe and F. Simon, 'Sneaking into school: Classroom history at work', in I. Grosvenor, M. Lawn and K. Rousmaniere (eds.), *Silences and Images* (New York: Peter Lang, 1999), pp. 13–46.

[48] In conducting the interviews general approaches used by qualitative researchers were utilized.

[49] See J. Kotre, *Outliving the Self: Generativity and the Interpretation of Lives* (Baltimore: Johns Hopkins University Press, 1984).

[50] By 'perspectives' is meant "frameworks through which people make sense of the world". See P. Woods, *Sociology and the School* (London: Routledge and Kegan Paul, 1983), p. 7.

[51] H. Silver, 'Nothing but the present, or nothing but the past', in P. Gordon (ed.), *The Study of Education: A Collection of Inaugural Lectures* (London: The Woburn Press, 1980), p. 267.

[52] See, for example, J. A. Hatch and R. Wisniewski, *Life History and Narrative* (London: The Falmer Press, 1995). See also K. Plummer, *Documents of Life* (Sydney: Allen and Unwin, 1983); R. Prus, *Symbolic Interaction and Ethnographic Research: Intersubjectivity and the Study of Human Lived Experience* (Albany: State University of New York Press, 1996), and G. Ritzer, *Sociological Theory* (New York: Alfred A. Knopf, 1994).

[53] D. Warren, 'Messages from the inside: Teachers as clues in history and policy', *International Journal of Educational Research*, Vol. 13, 1989, p. 379.

[54] R. Maclean and P. McKenzie, *Australian Teachers' Careers* (Victoria, Australia: Australian Council for Educational Research, 1991).

[55] I. V. Goodson and A. Hargreaves (eds.), *Teachers' Professional Lives* (London: Falmer Press, 1996).

[56] M. Huberman, *The Lives of Teachers* (London: Falmer Press, 1993).

Chapter Two

The Background

From the late 1800s until the early 1970s the majority of Catholic schools in Australia would hardly have survived had it not been for the large amount of cheap labor provided by teachers who were members of religious orders. So great was this provision that Catholic education during these years was dominated by nuns, religious brothers and priests. This chapter first of all outlines some general patterns in relation to such dominance. It then demonstrates that the various religious orders which ran the Catholic schools operated largely independently of each other. Both of these areas provide significant background to any account on what was distinctive about the process of education in Catholic schools in the country during the period 1922–65.

The Dominance of the Teaching Force in Catholic Schools by Members of Religious Orders

In the early part of the nineteenth century lay teachers and clerical teachers alike played a prominent part in the provision of Catholic education. The first religious orders arrived in the country in the 1830s.[1] Their major educational work in the early years was aimed at providing a basic primary school education for the Catholic population. Some of the male orders also attempted to replicate the aristocratic grammar school education provided by Protestant secondary schools.[2] Similarly, some of the female religious orders offered a 'culture and accomplishments' curriculum.[3] Abolition of state aid around the country in the latter half of the century, however, resulted in the view that the main function of Catholic primary schools was preserving the faith of its members and passing on its own distinctive cultural capital.[4] Catholic secondary schools, for the small number who progressed to them, also placed great emphasis on pupil preparation for public examinations so that the social and financial status of Catholics could be raised.[5]

The withdrawal of government financial assistance to Catholic schools in the latter half of the nineteenth century meant that lay teachers were no longer a viable option and so a large unpaid labor force was sought. To this end, individual Australian bishops were successful in persuading various religious orders from European Catholic countries to send more of their members to Australia in order to establish and staff schools. The first major surge in the growth of the religious orders in the country was in the 1880s. Irish religious orders constituted one group who made this possible because of a surplus of personnel relative to needs at home.[6] They were accompanied by continental-based orders, French in particular, motivated by a great new international missionary movement within the Church. The continental-based orders also sought locations such as Australia where they could work free from the sort of religious persecution they were experiencing at the hands of secularists at home.[7] A second surge came about in the early 1900s as the initial orders, which by now were well established, expanded the number of their convents, monasteries and houses around the country, and became prominent in schools, in orphanages, and in the care of the sick and aged.[8]

Over the next fifty years Catholic religious orders in Australia focused increasingly on education. By 1950, there were 44 orders in the country involved in teaching: 27 of nuns, 8 of religious brothers and 9 of priests. While the great majority of these orders originated overseas, 6 were uniquely Australian foundations: The Good Samaritan Sisters, the Sisters of Saint Joseph, the Sisters of Saint Joseph of the Most Sacred Heart of Jesus, the Home Missionary Sisters, the

Brothers of the Sacred Heart, and the Brothers of Saint John the Baptist.

In the latter half of the nineteenth century the Catholic Church in Australia, by insisting on having its own schools, reflected the mood of intransigent defiance of the Church as it responded internationally to what it saw as a hostile world. In other words, schools came to be seen by the Church as one of its instruments for holding on to, and reestablishing its control over, the faithful. In 1864, Pope Pius IX published his encyclical *Quanta Cura*, with its appended *Syllabus of Errors*, which included Proposition 48, condemning the idea that "Catholics may approve of that system of teaching youth which is separated from the Catholic faith and from ecclesiastical authority" and which "totally, or at least primarily, sees as its purpose the knowledge of natural science and of the social life of the world".[9] Five years later, when the Australian bishops met at the 'Second Provincial Council', this and the other education-related propositions from the *Syllabus* were included in their decrees, and members of the clergy were obliged to read and explain them to their parishioners.[10] Thus, as Praetz puts it, "the publication of the *Syllabus* enabled Catholic bishops to identify educational policy with fundamental dogma".[11]

In 1879 the bishops issued a 'joint pastoral letter' stating that Catholics must send their children to Catholic schools unless given special dispensation by their parish priest.[12] Over the next hundred years the bishops and the clergy regularly restated this position. The motivation for reiteration of such statements was the need of the clergy to reinforce its authority, as some Catholics chose, for whatever reasons, to send their children to state schools.[13] Nevertheless, the great majority of Catholics supported the Church's schools, particularly during the period 1922–65.

From about the mid 1880s to the mid 1950s, Catholic schooling, like government schooling, sought to keep pace with population growth. The outcome was both consolidation and expansion in an effort to provide a Catholic education for as many Catholic children as possible. The general pattern was one of around 17 per cent of all school-age pupils in the country being in Catholic schools. The ratio of primary to secondary school pupils in Catholic schools largely reflected the situation in government schools, reaching a ratio of two-to-one at the end of the 1960s. Catholic secondary schools in the cities and larger towns were single sex institutions, with boys' schools being staffed almost totally by priests or brothers, and girls' schools being staffed by nuns. In some cases primary schools were co-educational until the last two-to-three years, when boys transferred from a school run by nuns to one run by brothers or priests. By contrast, the rural areas were dotted with small two- and three-teacher coeducational primary schools, usually staffed by nuns only, generally Sisters of Mercy, Sisters of Saint Joseph of the Most Sacred Heart of Jesus, Sisters of Saint Joseph, Dominican Sisters, or Presentation Sisters.

Catholic pupils and their parents were constantly reminded that their schools were different because they were a different type of people. This notion of difference was celebrated in the following popular melody recalled by Campion:

> I am a little Catholic;
> I love my Holy Faith;
> I will be true to Holy Church,
> And steadfast unto death.
>
> I shun the schools of those who seek
> To snare poor Catholic youth;
> No Church I own—no schools I know,
> But those that teach the truth.[14]

Some of the differences which existed between Catholic schools and other schools in the country related to the process of education, the subject of the remaining chapters of this book. However, there were also differences in the work of teachers; differences which arose out of the fact that Catholic teachers were members of religious orders and were expected to commit themselves totally to their work by taking on many more duties than would be considered reasonable for a state school teacher, or for a lay teacher in a Catholic school. These included cleaning the school, care of the surroundings, training school teams, provision (without payment) of extra tuition for 'slow learners', conduct of the work of the various religious 'sodalities' for pupils and adults, organization of school concerts, engagement in a variety of fund-raising activities, and preparation of pupils for the Sacraments of Confession, Communion and Confirmation. In the larger metropolitan schools and the small country boarding schools the same teachers often supervised boarders after school and at weekends. In many cases nuns, particularly those from orders teaching the poorer sections of society, had to give music lessons and speech lessons after school hours in order to supplement the income which their particular communities derived from low school fees.

Beginning in the 1930s, there was an increase in the demands made of teachers in Catholic schools as the school leaving age rose. Concurrently, the promotion of government policy of 'education for all' led to the expectation of a similar commitment from the non-government educational sector.[15] The 1940s witnessed a trend to earlier marriage, to an increasing proportion of women marrying, and to an increase in migration.[16] A consequence in the early 1950s was that all schools struggled to meet the challenge of a rapidly growing school population. The response of overworked teachers in Catholic schools with larger classes was rigid control and routine discipline. Now also these teachers encountered large numbers of children whose first language was not English because of the government's migration policy which attracted Southern Europeans, many of whom were Catholics.

The following is the general pattern of increase in the number of religious-order teachers in the country between 1900 and 1950:

Table 2.1: No. of Religious-Order Teachers in Each State: 1900–1950

State	1900	1910	1920	1930	1940	1950
New South Wales	2004	2688	3515	4325	4798	5601
Victoria	786	1414	1689	2031	2564	2701
South Australia	284	389	430	582	676	796
Western Australia	173	416	581	617	1206	1284
Queensland	299	395	763	1205	1719	1993
Tasmania	119	135	174	197	227	302
Total	3665	5437	7152	8957	11190	12677

Source: R. Fogarty, *Catholic Education in Australia: 1806–1950*, p. 278.

What these figures show is a gradual increase in membership of religious orders in each state during each decade. What they do not reveal, however, is that within the religious orders, nuns greatly exceeded their male counterparts, thus continuing a trend of the previous century.[17]

The extent of the dominance of nuns over religious brothers and priests in the Catholic teaching force throughout the first five decades of the twentieth century can be represented thus:

Table 2.2: No. of Nuns, Brothers and Priests Teaching: 1900–1950

Year	Nuns	Brothers	Priests	Total
1900	3059	379	53	3491
1910	5081	466	53	5600
1920	6571	634	51	7246
1930	8277	778	61	9116
1940	10149	1041	84	11274
1950	11245	1532	124	12901

Source: R. Fogarty, *Catholic Education in Australia: 1806–1950*, p. 270.

This situation meant that nuns dominated the total teaching force in all Catholic schools combined, both primary and secondary, throughout the period.

It has not been possible to establish the exact number of nuns within each order teaching in Catholic schools in Australia throughout the period 1922–65. It is possible, however, to get some idea of the relative involvement in teaching of the different orders from their total numbers. The following table outlines the situation for Australia as a whole for 1930 and 1960 for those orders which were most prominent in teaching:

Table 2.3: No. of Nuns in Major Teaching Orders in Australia

Order	1930	1960
Sisters of Mercy	2794	3949
Sisters of St. Joseph of the Most Sacred Heart	979	1742
Sisters of St. Joseph	540	575
Presentation Sisters	529	926
Sisters of the Good Samaritan	446	619
Dominican Sisters	262	641
Sisters of Charity	372	476
Sisters of St. Brigid	231	420
Loreto Sisters	205	227
O.L.S.H. Sisters	138	275

Source: *The Australasian Catholic Record* for the years 1930 and 1960.

While the largest of these orders were also involved in other work, including nursing, this pattern still gives some indication of the extent to which Catholic education was dominated by eight of them, and particularly by the Sisters of Mercy, the Sisters of Saint Joseph of the Most Sacred Heart of Jesus, the Sisters of Saint Joseph, and the Presentation Sisters.

The number of religious brothers, while never remotely approaching that of nuns, continued to outnumber greatly the number of priests teaching in the schools, most of whom were also members of religious orders rather than diocesan priests. The situation in the Catholic dioceses in Western Australia was as follows:

Table 2.4: No. of Nuns and Brothers Teaching in Western Australia

Year	No. of Nuns Teaching	No. of Religious Brothers Teaching
1930	567	29
1940	910	48
1950	967	63
1960	1052	93
1970	1075	116

Source: *The Australasian Catholic Record* for the years 1930 and 1960.

As with nuns, the exact national figures for those brothers within each teaching order who were teaching in Catholic schools between 1922 and 1965 could not be established. Again, however, it is possible to get some idea of the relative involvement of the different teaching orders from their total numbers. The situation in 1930 and 1960 was as follows:

Table 2.5: No. of Brothers in Major Teaching Orders in Australia

Order	1930	1960
Christian Brothers	374	800
Marist Brothers	180	342
De La Salle Brothers	43	200
Patrician Brothers	25	49

Source: *The Australasian Catholic Record* for the years 1930 and 1960.

From these figures it is clear that throughout the period the Christian Brothers outnumbered the total number of all of those in the other major orders of teaching brothers combined.

As in the two preceding categories, it has not been possible to determine the exact number of priests in religious orders who were teachers. Nevertheless, some idea of the relative involvement of the different teaching orders of priests can be gained from their total numbers. The situation in 1930 and 1960 was thus:

Table 2.6: No. of Priests in Major Teaching Orders in Australia

Order	1930	1960
Jesuits	70	169
Marist Fathers	19	168
Missionaries of The Sacred Heart	66	161
Franciscan Fathers	15	108
Dominican Priests	18	50

Source: *The Australasian Catholic Record* for the years 1930 and 1960.

All told, the number of priests, as with the number of lay people, in the Catholic teaching force, was tiny in comparison to both the number of nuns and religious brothers.

Overall, then, for the period 1922–65, nuns constituted the most visible group of teachers in Catholic education in Australia, particularly in the primary schools, where they taught both boys and girls. It is true that in the larger centers of population boys often moved to a school run by a male religious order—usually the Christian Brothers—for the last two years of primary schooling. The majority of Catholic children, however, like other Australian children, did not proceed to secondary schooling. This meant that the majority of Catholic Australians, both male and female, received most of their education from teachers who were not just members of religious orders, but who also happened to be nuns. Thus, when it is pointed out that one of the most notable changes in Catholic schools from the 1960s was the gradual replacement of the teaching orders by Catholic lay teachers,[18] it needs to be kept in mind that the great majority who were being replaced were nuns.

Finally, a particularly significant consequence of the dominance of Catholic schools by teachers who were members of religious orders, both male and female, arose out of the fact that they themselves had experienced an extensive program of 'religious training'. Much of the next chapter is concerned with outlining and demonstrating how this training program influenced the approach of nuns, religious brothers and priests to teaching. Before coming to it, however, it is necessary to have some understanding of the basic administrative framework within which religious orders in Australia operated.

The Degree of Independence of the Religious Teaching Orders

The major administrative unit of the Catholic Church throughout the world is the diocese, which is overseen by a bishop. By the end of the period 1922–65 there were twenty-eight dioceses in Australia. In the great majority of cases these were sub-divisions of the country's States and Territories.

A diocese is sub-divided into parishes. The principal work of the Church at this level is carried out by diocesan priests whose main task is to preach, catechise and administer the sacraments. During the period 1922–65 the only teaching which the diocesan priests normally did in schools was when they occasionally visited to give a special lesson in religious instruction. They did, however, have a duty to establish, wherever possible, a local parish primary school and then, through the bishop, to get a religious order to come and staff it with nuns, religious brothers, or priests who were members of religious orders. These schools complemented those owned by the religious orders. Broadly speaking, then, we can speak of the orders running and staffing two types of school, the parochial school and the order-owned school.

In the case of the parochial schools, the land, school buildings, facilities, servicing, upkeep, budgetary allowances and financial control were, legally and practically, the responsibility of the parish priest, as were many aspects of school policy, including enrolments, staff composition and class sizes. Bourke summarized the pattern of the early formation and spreading of these schools:

> A parish primary school came to be recognized as the normal way for the Church to discharge for the children of the parish community, its obligations of religious education. Three conditions needed to be met for the foundation of the school: a sufficient number of children; funds available (usually on loan) to provide classrooms; and a religious order

able and willing to undertake the provision of staff. When these conditions
could be met, a parish primary school could be set up. In hundreds of cases
this was possible, and the result was a network of primary schools. [19]

Where parishes had a large number of children, secondary
departments were added to existing primary schools; often one such
department served a 'catchment area' which had several small
primary schools.[20] These secondary departments were also supplied
with teachers from a religious order, but the school remained vested
in the diocese or parish. The majority of secondary schools, however,
were order-owned schools.

Church protocol ensured that no religious order made an initial
foundation of a parochial school or an order-owned school within
a diocese without the permission of the local bishop, although once
they had established themselves within a diocese some of the orders
went on to set up their own order-owned schools. As Turner puts it,
"a religious congregation would often build a convent or monastery
on its privately owned land and then proceed to open private primary
and secondary schools, usually with a boarding section attached".[21]
While the religious personnel staffing the parochial schools were,
because of their financial independence, concerned solely with
teaching and with day-to-day administrative matters, those in the
order-owned schools were able to exercise a high degree of initiative
in planning a school's development.

To date, very little research has been undertaken on the relative
social and cultural effects of the order-run schools and the parochial
schools. A useful starting point in initiating such research would be to
focus on Turner's[22] argument that the parochial schools catered to
the poorer children while the more well-to-do attended order-run
schools where they paid higher fees. Certainly, particular religious
orders, especially the Jesuits,[23] the Loreto Sisters and the Sisters of the
Sacred Heart, catered to the upper echelons of Catholic society, while
the Christian Brothers and the Sisters of Mercy catered to those at
the lower level of the social ladder. Also, a certain amount
of snobbery emerged within the Catholic education sector and was
reflected in the social distancing created by such practices as the
labeling of the better-off schools rather grandiosely as 'colleges'.

At the same time, however, while some religious orders concentrated their efforts exclusively on teaching the Catholic middle classes, others catered to a wider spectrum of society. Within some cities there were certain Christian Brothers' schools which vied with their Jesuit-like counterparts in terms of the social-class origins of their pupils, while not far away were other Christian Brothers' schools which catered mainly to boys from less well-off homes. Equally, in some cases the Sisters of Mercy even had two schools on a single campus, one school which was fee-paying for those who could afford to pay and another which did not charge fees for those who could not. Accordingly, there are grounds for maintaining that Turner's argument is a sweeping over-generalization and that the pattern was a more complex one which can only be revealed through further detailed research.

The pattern in the ways in which the different religious orders were governed is, by contrast, very clear. What this pattern reveals is the level of independence which the individual orders had both of each other and of the authorities of the dioceses in which they and their schools were located. Furthermore, such independence meant that no major structure existed throughout the period 1922–65 for the systematic long-term planning which would have been required to build a coordinated Catholic education system. Such a structure could have encouraged a sharing of resources and resulted in greater economies than pertained in situations where a number of religious orders operated schools within close proximity, yet quite independently of one another.

Two broad divisions existed within the religious orders in Australia, namely, pontifical orders and diocesan orders. The pontifical orders operated almost exclusively under the governing authority of their own superiors, with minimum reference to the diocesan bishop. This often meant governance through a superior-general at the international level, a provincial superior at the level of the region or province, and a local superior at the monastery or convent level. All of the male religious orders involved in education in Australia operated under this pontifical model, as did some of the female orders, most notably the Sisters of Saint Joseph of the Most Sacred Heart of Jesus and the Loreto Sisters.

The Christian Brothers, with the largest number of schools for boys in Australia during 1922–65, is a pontifical order. Towards the end of the period the order was governed by a 'general council' in Rome, consisting of a Superior General and four assistants. Each of these assistants represented four groups of provinces. The first group consisted of two Irish provinces and one English province; the second group consisted of two provinces in the United States and one province in Canada; the third group consisted of one South African province and one Indian province; and the fourth group consisted of one New Zealand province and four Australian provinces. The governance structure of the four Australian provinces was organized geographically as follows: (1) New South Wales/New Guinea; (2) Victoria/Tasmania; (3) Western Australia/South Australia; and (4) Queensland. This structure serves to demonstrate how the administrative boundaries of national or international religious orders within the country did not always correspond with diocesan boundaries. For instance, the Western Australian/South Australian province (Holy Spirit Province), embracing twenty schools in 1975, extended across six different dioceses. The replication of this type of situation around Australia in the case of the different pontifical religious orders meant that they did not negotiate or work with each other or with diocesan orders in an effort to organize Catholic education in the country along neat administrative lines. Consequently, it is not surprising that from the early 1800s, various conflicts, tensions, misunderstandings and lack of effective communication developed between bishops and the governing authorities of the pontifical religious orders over the administration of Catholic schools in Australia.

A number of female orders were also diocesan congregations. Under the diocesan model, when a female order established its first convent in a diocese it became known as the diocese's 'mother house'. This, in turn, often led to branch houses being formed. Sometimes these branch houses themselves became independent houses in their own right, then went on to form their own branch houses. The standard justification of such a model at the time was that it gave greater flexibility to diocesan orders than to pontifical orders to respond to local demands. For example, if they wanted to establish a school, orphanage or hospital, or initiate a social services project, the diocesan orders could do so within a short period without having to submit proposals and plans through a hierarchical bureaucratic framework of governance. At the same time, it has also been contended that members of diocesan orders were not as exposed to ideas and trends developing elsewhere as were members of pontifical orders, that they did not have anything like the same mobility, and that they tended to be subject "to the dangers of narrowness, isolation and inbreeding".[24]

Within a diocesan order the jurisdiction of the superior of each group under one 'mother house' was limited to that group within the diocese. The superior, in turn, came under the direct authority of the bishop of the diocese. This pattern of development had led to such a proliferation of different groups within individual diocesan orders by the early part of the twentieth century that a number of them amalgamated for reasons of efficiency. The complexity of the situation can be illustrated by outlining the position in Western Australia:

Table 2.7: Religious Order Schools in Western
Australia in 1950, Dating Time of Arrival in the State

Religious Order	Arrived in WA	Diocesan Order	Pontifical Order
Sisters of Mercy	1846	x	
Presentation Sisters	1891	x	
Sisters of St. Joseph of the Apparition	1855		x
Sisters of St. Joseph of the Most Sacred Heart	1887		x
Sisters of Our Lady of the Missions	1897		x
Loreto Sisters	1897		x
Dominican Sisters	1899		x
Brigidine Sisters	1942		x
Schoenstatt Sisters	1951		x
Ursuline Sisters	1955		x
Christian Brothers	1894		x
De La Salle Brothers	1864		x
Marist Brothers	1913		x
Vincentian Fathers	1948		x

Source: *The Australasian Catholic Record* for the years in question.

Here it can be seen that the Sisters of Mercy and the Presentation Sisters were the only two diocesan orders in the state. Yet, between them they had by far the greatest number of members. Consequently, as the following table demonstrates, they also controlled almost half of the Catholic schools run by nuns in the state in 1955:

Table 2.8: Catholic Schools Run
by Nuns in Western Australia in 1955

Religious Order	No. of Schools
Sisters of Mercy	37
Presentation Sisters	19
Sisters of St. Joseph of the Most Sacred Heart	18
Dominican Sisters	12
Sisters of Our Lady of the Missions	10
Sisters of St. Joseph of the Apparition	9
Loreto Sisters	4
The Brigidine Sisters	3
The Ursuline Sisters	1
The Schoenstatt Sisters	1

Source: *The Australasian Catholic Record* for 1955.

This table does not allow for the fact that within Mercy Sisters and the Presentations Sisters there were further sub-divisions. The thirty-seven Mercy schools consisted of 28 schools of the Sisters of Mercy Perth and nine schools of the West Perth Mercy Sisters. The nineteen Presentation schools consisted of the ten schools of the Geraldton Presentation Sisters and the nine schools of the Iona (Perth) Presentation Sisters.

Between them, the Sisters of Mercy and the Presentation Sisters were also the only two religious orders of nuns involved in educational provision in all of the ecclesiastical districts in the state, namely, the Archdiocese of Perth, the Diocese of Geraldton, the Diocese of Bunbury, the Diocese of New Norcia, and the Vicariate of the Kimberley, which became the Diocese of Broome in 1966. This is illustrated in the following table which outlines the geographical pattern of educational provision by nuns in each of these five districts in Western Australia in 1955:

Table 2.9: Geographical Pattern of Educational Provision by
Nuns in the Ecclesiastical Districts in Western Australia in 1955

Nuns	Perth	Geraldton	Bunbury	New Norcia	Kimberley
Presentation Sisters	x	x	x	x	x
Sisters of Saint Joseph of the Most Sacred Heart	x	x	x		
Sisters of Mercy	x		x		
Sisters of Saint Joseph of the Apparition	x		x		
Sisters of Our Lady of the Mission	x		x		
Dominican Sister	x	x			
Schoenstatt Sister	x	x			
Loreto Sisters	x				
Brigidine Sisters	x				
Ursuline Sisterrs	x				
Oblate Benedictines				x	
John of God Sisters					x

Source: *The Australasian Catholic Record* for 1955.

Furthermore, as the following brief account of the development of the Sisters of Mercy in Western Australia demonstrates, they are classic examples of the way in which diocesan orders sometimes established mother houses in the one state quite independently of each other, went on to form branches, and then, at a later stage, regrouped in various ways.

Of the orders of teaching sisters in Western Australia during the period 1922–65, the Sisters of Mercy was the largest.[25] This order was also the first to arrive in the state, coming from Baggot Street in Dublin in 1846. Over the years it spread through the establishment of various separate and autonomous foundations. By the 1950s it was common to hear people speak of two branches: the Sisters of Mercy Perth, focused on the original foundation at Victoria Square, and the West Perth Mercy Sisters.

The evolution of the Sisters of Mercy Perth is the more complicated of the two divisions. From the initial foundation of Irish Sisters in Victoria Square, branch convents were established at

Guildford (1855), York (1872) and Toodyay (1884). In 1900, these branch convents became independent communities. During 1911 and 1912, in response to directives from Rome, there was a re-amalgamation of these foundations with the original Victoria Square foundation, and they became known at the Sisters of Mercy Perth. Meanwhile, the Sisters of Mercy Bunbury had been founded from Victoria Square in 1897 as a separate foundation and set up its own branch houses. Other separate foundations of Mercy Sisters were those at Coolgardie, founded from Adelaide in 1898, and at Victoria Park, Perth, founded from Derry, Ireland, in 1899. During the 1930s these various foundations amalgamated with the Sisters of Mercy Perth: in 1934 the Sisters of Mercy Victoria Park was incorporated with the Sisters of Mercy Perth; in 1936, the Sisters of Mercy Bunbury amalgamated with the Sisters of Mercy Perth to form an entity called 'The Sisters of Mercy Perth Amalgamated'; and in 1938, the Sisters of Mercy Coolgardie was incorporated with this entity. By 1955, the 'Sisters of Mercy Perth Amalgamated' had 248 sisters in all, was responsible for 28 schools in the Archdiocese of Perth and the Diocese of Bunbury, was also responsible for St. Joseph's Orphanage in Wembley and St. Anne's General and Maternity Hospital in Mt. Lawley, and was concerned with regular visitation of the poor and the sick. It, along with seven other self-governing communities, decided in 1954 to form the Australian Union of the Sisters of Mercy, which was then divided into provinces under a common superior.

The evolution of the other major division originated with the Sisters of Mercy at West Perth, founded from Victoria Square in 1898. This foundation ultimately developed its own branch houses at Leederville, Lesmurdie, Osborne Park and Kojonup and, in 1955, was responsible for nine schools. It was one of nine Australian congregations which, wishing to retain autonomy in government, did not join the Australian Union of the Sisters of Mercy in 1954, but instead formed a federation in 1956.

Around Australia similar amalgamations took place amongst other religious orders, including the Presentation Sisters,[26] the Dominican Sisters, the Sisters of Saint Joseph and the Poor Clare Sisters. Also, a certain degree of cooperation on educational matters between religious orders themselves (both pontifical and diocesan) and between orders and diocesan authorities was underway. The origins of such cooperation went back to the 1920s, when individual bishops began appointing a priest to a diocesan Catholic education office, with the main function of supervising and assisting the specifically religious elements of the work of the schools in the diocese. Appointees to these offices were not usually involved in the financial administration of education. Before long, however, they began to advocate greater coordination in the work of schools. By 1936, priests attached to education offices around the country were sufficiently committed to this notion that they met in Adelaide to discuss it in detail and to make recommendations to the nation's bishops.[27] Two of their recommendations were accepted at the Third Plenary Council held in Sydney in 1937. The first of these was that in each diocese an inspector of schools be appointed and that he (sic) be delegated to act in respect to certain specific areas in relation to schools, while the second was that a conference of directors and inspectors be held every three years, beginning in 1938.[28]

Bourke[29] notes that, over time, the diocesan education offices progressively gathered other tasks: "They acted as representatives for schools as centers of information, as starting points for consultation and co-ordination between schools, as sources of help in lifting the quality of teaching in secular as well as religious subjects". By the late 1940s and early 1950s, the various orders in each diocese, which had previously worked almost totally independently of each other, began to communicate more with each other and engage in some cooperation in education, including mounting various joint courses on the teaching of religion and other school subjects.[30] Similarly on the national scene, the work of the Bishops' Committee for Education, a committee of the Australian Episcopal Conference, also increased. Its principal initial concern was the development of a series of religious texts, with the first volume being published in 1962. The committee also began to be drawn increasingly into the examination of policy and practice regarding the religious education of children both within and beyond Catholic schools.

The stirring of some cooperation between the various groups involved in Catholic education in Australia was driven largely by those who pointed out the duplication of facilities created by too many small schools within close proximity of each other. The impetus for greater cooperation accelerated with the crisis in enrolments in the 1950s and 1960s. The inspectors of Catholic schools began to emphasize the disadvantages inherent in the lack of co-ordination between the different sectors of Catholic education. In the Archdiocese of Perth, for example, the Director of Catholic Education, Monsignor James Bourke,[31] highlighted the hindrances to cooperation caused by the diffusion of authority as follows:

> While each are co-operating in the same field, there is in practice a good deal of mutual lack of trust and a mutual attempt to protect individual interests. This makes concerted effort and any form of central decision on almost any problem an extremely difficult business. Most of the people involved are so busy that effective and sustained consultation is not possible.

By now it was also possible to legitimate such concerns by reference to developments within the Church internationally. For example, the First International Congress of Religious in Rome in 1950 marked the beginning of a movement towards considering the needs and problems of the religious orders in the light of modern circumstances. This movement reached Australia through a series of separate congresses for brothers and sisters of Australia, New Zealand and Oceania, the first of which was held in Sydney in 1955, and all of which helped to promote a desire for fuller co-ordination and collaboration amongst the orders.[32]

Various recommendations of the congresses were put into effect. University attendance by some members of religious orders increased as a result of a recommendation that there should be an improvement in the quality and level of education of nuns, religious brothers and priests teaching in schools, including the quality of their teacher education. The congresses also helped to promote consultation between the different religious orders involved in education and bring about a realization of the need for forward planning, the elimination of wasteful duplication, and the sharing of facilities and expert knowledge.[33]

This growing level of cooperation within the Church on Catholic education grew as the Second Vatican Council got underway in 1962.

A new spirit of openness generated by the council also encouraged debate on the nature of Catholic education in Australia. For example, some criticisms from within the Church of the uncritical adoption of state curricula by Catholic schools were voiced along the following lines:

> There are just close on 15,000 religious teaching in Australia at present, but their impact on education generally has been very slight. They have not come forward with sustained criticisms of existing educational philosophies; they have not provided alternative curricula of their own, but have conformed to a pattern which in principle presumably they do not approve. Catholic schools have been carried on barely at subsistence level in many cases and there has not been the time or opportunity to stand back and examine the position in the light of changed historical circumstances.[34]

Others went so far as to question the very existence of Catholic education:

> Both the 'saving of souls' and the 'teaching of the catechism' are inadequate as reasons for the existence of Catholic schools. There is nothing, in fact, in Catholic principles that makes a separate system absolutely necessary. Have we, here in Australia, rethought our position [since the nineteenth century] and taken more than the first step along the road to a justification of our schools in terms of the present day? Do we still basically think of our schools as existing to 'save souls' or 'teach the catechism' with a narrow interpretation of what these mean? If we do, then we may be confusing the role of the school with that of education in general.[35]

While such thinking did not lead to a dismantling of Catholic education, it did contribute to major reconsideration and reform of the principles underlying Catholic schooling. In order to consider these developments, however, it would be necessary to go beyond the parameters of this book. Instead, it is now appropriate to move on to the first of four chapters which deal with the central area of concern, namely, what was distinctive about Catholic education in Australia during the period 1922–65.

Notes

Table 2.10: Religious Orders taking up Teaching in Australia:1830 to 1950

Decade	Priests
1830s	Benedictine Fathers
1840s	Marist Fathers; Jesuit Fathers
1860s	Assumptionist Fathers
1870s	Augustinian Fathers
1880s	Vincentian Fathers; Missionaries of the Sacred Heart
1890s	Holy Ghost Fathers
1920s	Salesian Fathers
Decade	**Religious Brothers**
1840s	Irish Christian Brothers
1860s	De La Salle Brothers
1870s	Marist Brothers; Brothers of The Sacred Heart
1880s	Patrician Brothers
1890s	Franciscan Brothers
1910s	Brothers of St. John the Baptist
1940s	Brothers of St. John of God
Decade	**Female Religious**
1830s	Sisters of Charity
1840s	Sisters of Mercy; Brigidine Sisters
1850s	Sisters of St. Joseph of the Apparition; Good Samaritan Sisters
1860s	Good Shepherd Sisters;
	Sisters of St. Joseph of the Most Sacred Heart of Jesus;
	Dominican Sisters; Presentation Sisters
1870s	Sisters of St. Joseph; Loreto Sisters
1880s	Ursuline Sisters; Dominican Sisters (3rd Order)
	Faithful Companions of Jesus; Religious of the Sacred Heart;
	Brigidine Sisters;
	Poor Clare Sisters;
	Daughters of the Sacred Heart
1890s	Sisters of Notre Dame de Sion;
	Sisters of St. John of God;
	Sisters of Notre Dame des Mission
1900s	Marist Sisters
1930s	Franciscan Sisters of the Immaculate Conception
1940s	Sisters of Compassion;
	Sisters of St. Joseph of California;
	Home Missionary Sisters

Source: R. Fogarty, *Catholic Education in Australia: 1806–1950*, p. 270.

It is clear from this table that a greater variety of female religious orders were involved in teaching in Australia over the period in question than male religious orders. Also, it is clear that the majority of all religious orders who came to Australia had arrived in the country by 1900.

[2] See A. G. Maclaine, *Australian Education: Progress, Problems and Prospects* (Sydney: Ian Novak, 1973), p. 148.

[3] Ibid., p. 149.

[4] See A. Potts, 'Public and private schooling in Australia: Some historical and contemporary considerations', *Phi Delta Kappan*, Nov. 1999, p. 241.

[5] See N. Turner, *Catholics in Australia: A Social History, Vol. 1* (Victoria, Australia: Collins Dove, 1992), pp. 229–249.

[6] See R. Fogarty, *Catholic Education in Australia: 1806–1950* (Melbourne: Melbourne University Press, 1959), pp. 257–303.

[7] Ibid.

[8] Ibid.

[9] Cited in J. Molony, *The Roman Mould of the Australian Catholic Church* (Melbourne: Melbourne University Press, 1969), p. 111.

[10] See P. J. O'Farrell (ed.), *Documents in Australian Catholic History, Vol. 1* (London: Geoffrey Chapman, 1969), p. 396.

[11] H. Praetz, *Where Shall We Send Them? The Choice of School for a Catholic Child* (Melbourne: Melbourne University Press, 1974), p. 3.

[12] See A. Potts, 'Public and private schooling in Australia: Some historical and contemporary considerations', p. 245.

[13] For example, in 1884 somewhere between one-half and one-third of Catholic children in New South Wales did not attend Catholic schools. By the mid-1930s about one- ninth of Melbourne's Catholic school children were not in Catholic schools, but the overall figure for Australia remained at about one-third of Catholic children outside the Catholic education sector. See N. Turner, *Catholics in Australia: A Social History, Vol. 1* (Victoria, Australia: Collins Dove, 1992), p. 231.

[14] E. Campion, 'Irish religion in Australia', *The Australasian Catholic Record*, Vol. 55, 1978, p. 15.

[15] See A. G. Maclaine, *Australian Education: Progress, Problems and Prospects*, p. 149.

[16] Ibid.

[17] U. Corrigan, 'The achievements of the Catholic people of Australia in the field of education', in Australian Catholic Education Congress, *Australian Catholic Education Congress: Adelaide. Australia, 1936* (Melbourne: The Advocate Press, 1936), pp. 292–294. Here we are told that the number of nuns in Australia increased to 8,500 between 1885 and 1935, while the number of Brothers only reached 950 over the same period

[18] By 1969 the proportion of lay teachers in Catholic schools ranged from 30 per cent in Western Australia to almost 46 per cent in Victoria. The figures for the other states were 44 per cent in New South Wales, 38 per cent in Queensland, 35 per cent in South Australia and 36 per cent in Tasmania. The increase in the number of lay teachers has continued up to the present time. By the early 1980s the proportion of lay to religious teachers was 90 per cent to 10 per cent, respectively, with the gap increasing further in the 1990s. This has not

resulted in a decline in numbers attending Catholic schools, or in the status of the schools themselves, whether determined by criteria relating to scholastic success or the fulfillment of their spiritual, moral and religious ideals.

[19] J. E. Bourke, 'Roman Catholic schools', in D. A. Jecks (ed.), *Influences in Australian Education* (Perth, Australia: Carroll's, 1974), p. 257.

[20] Ibid.

[21] See N. Turner, *Catholics in Australia: A Social History, Vol. 1*, p. 234.

[22] Ibid. p. 235.

[23] See G. Dening and D. Kennedy, *Xavier Portraits* (Melbourne: Old Xavierians' Association, 1993), pp. 121–123.

[24] M. C. Leavey, 'Religious education, school climate and achievement: A study of nine Catholic sixth-form girls' schools' (unpublished Ph.D. thesis, Australian National University, 1972), p. 21.

[25] This account is based on that in A. Tormey, *Teaching Orders in Catholic Education in Western Australia 1955–1975: A Historical Study of Changes and Repercussions* (unpublished M.Ed. thesis, The University of Western Australia, 1976).

[26] The first group was focused on a foundation made from Ireland in Geraldton in 1891. By the 1950s it was responsible for ten schools in the Geraldton Diocese. The other foundation centred on the Iona Convent in Mosman Park, Perth, and was founded from Wagga Wagga in 1900. By the 1950s it was responsible for three city schools and six parochial country schools in the Archdiocese of Perth. Also during the 1950s efforts were made to unite the different Presentation Congregations in Australia. As a result, on 8 January 1958, Pope Pius XII formally established a Society of Congregations of the Sisters of the Presentation of the Blessed Virgin Mary, granting permission for any Presentation congregation to join the society. When the society was officially inaugurated on 11 April, 1958, the Geraldton congregation was one of the six members, while the Perth Congregation joined in 1965.

[27] J. E. Bourke, 'Roman Catholic schools', p. 257.

[28] Ibid., p. 258.

[29] Ibid.

[30] Ibid., p. 260.

[31] See A. Tormey, *Teaching Orders in Catholic Education in Western Australia 1955–1975: A Historical Study of Changes and Repercussions*, p. 12.

[32] Ibid., p. 14.

[33] See A. G. Maclaine, *Australian Education: Progress, Problems and Prospects*, p. 155.

[34] M. C. Leavey, 'The relevance of St. Thomas Aquinas for Australian education', in E. L. French (ed.), *Melbourne Studies in Education* (Melbourne: Melbourne University Press, 1964), p. 299.

[35] Quoted in N. Turner, *Catholics in Australia: A Social History, Vol. 2* (Victoria, Australia: Collins Dove, 1992), p. 111.

Chapter Three

The Authoritarian Nature of Catholic Schooling

One of the major characteristics of the process of education in Catholic schools in Australia from 1922 to 1965 was that it was conducted within an authoritarian framework. At one level, this was no more than a reflection of the situation in government schools; Connell contends that in the early 1960s, the traditional primary school throughout Australia, regardless of whether one is referring to the government or the non-government sector, was "characterised by orderliness, careful teacher control and direction, and an emphasis on the 3Rs".[1] Catholic schools stood out in this regard because of the inflexible approach of teachers working within such parameters. To develop an understanding of this situation it is necessary to focus on the nature of the life of those who were members of the Catholic teaching force during this time period; a teaching force made up almost entirely of nuns, religious brothers and priests, with the number of nuns greatly exceeding that of their male colleagues.

This chapter commences with an exposition on what was distinctive about the life of teachers who were members of Catholic religious orders. The particular thrust of the exposition is on the authoritarian framework within which they were 'formed' for a life based on an observance of the vows of poverty, chastity and obedience. The chapter then presents an account demonstrating that the program of personal 'formation' based upon this framework needs to be kept in mind when considering the more specific teacher training received by those who were members of Catholic religious orders. Finally, attention is given to how the authoritarian framework extended to the conduct of the schools, thus ensuring that the habitual ways in which the members of religious orders were taught to think and act were not threatened when they became fully-fledged members of the Catholic teaching force.

The Distinctiveness of the Life of Catholic Teachers Who Were Members of Religious Orders

In the early days of Catholic education in Australia the schools were run largely by lay teachers. Gradually, they were replaced by nuns, religious brothers and priests, until by the end of the nineteenth and the beginning of the twentieth century the religious orders came to dominate the teaching force. Initially, the orders were brought in to the country so that a mass system of education could be run at minimum expense. Over the years, however, their presence came to be legitimated by the Church on other grounds. Fogarty summarizes the general view which came to be articulated:

> Given the non-Catholic environment of Australia and the consequent greater need for a positively Catholic environment in the Catholic school, the bishops had consistently preferred religious. The selection of religious in the first place, then their years of preparation and regular periods for the renewal of the spirit, conferred on them, it was generally believed, a special stamp.[2]

Largely, the argument was that the 'religious personality' of the teacher who was a member of a religious order rendered him or her ideally suited for shaping young Catholic minds. What is being referred to here, of course, is not one's 'natural' personality but, rather, the personality which was formed through a period of special religious training, of which teacher training was an integral part.

Against this background, lay teachers, who were very much a minority in the schools, were marginalized. The nature of the rhetoric, regulations and practices which sanctioned this marginalization provides insights regarding the self-image of those in religious life, particularly the way in which they were psychologically oriented to consider themselves to be much more suitable for teaching than were lay people. For example, in excluding lay teachers from the development of school policy, the standard argument of the nuns, religious brothers and priests was that they themselves were eminently more suited to determining policy and administering the schools because of their religious commitment, their total devotion to their work, and the fact that they were not distracted by family demands and problems.

In considering this further it is important to keep in mind that members of religious orders lived in communities so that they could, as the 'Rules' of the Christian Brothers put it, "reduce within the bounds of Christian charity all those sentiments for relations with which flesh and blood would inspire them". The particular rule went on to say that "it is not sufficient that the body quits the world, the heart also must break off all attachment thereto".[3] In a similar vein, the 'Constitutions of the Sisters of Mercy' stated that the "general object" of the order was "the glory of God and the personal sanctification of its members by means of the observance of the three simple vows of poverty, chastity and obedience".[4] Various safeguards were instituted by the different religious orders to facilitate the attainment of such objectives. One such safeguard was embodied in those rules and regulations of the orders which made explicit the need for their members to distance themselves from the lay teachers. The reasoning behind this was that lay teachers were 'seculars' and that "it is by unnecessary communication with seculars, that the religious spirit departs from Communities, and that the spirit of the world enters with its train of abuses and relaxation".[5] On this, the Loreto 'Rules' simply stated that no sister was to speak with seculars, "or call others to speak with them, without a particular or general leave of the Superior".[6] Other religious orders, however, were more explicit, particularly in highlighting what were perceived to be the dangers involved. For example, the *Guide for the Sisters of Mercy* stated:

> All who have experience in the direction of religious, as well as those who have written for their instruction, concur in declaring unnecessary secular intercourse most prejudicial to their perfection.[7]

The Presentation Sisters also were instructed to "maintain the most guarded reserve" when dealing with 'seculars' and never to be "in the least degree familiar".[8] Along similar lines, the *Directory and Rules of the Christian Brothers* required members to "abstain from frequent and unnecessary conversations with seculars" and to avoid "engaging in political conversations with assistant teachers".[9] By 'assistant teachers' was meant lay teachers. What was being made clear through this terminology was that a lay teacher was to be employed in a school only when no nun, religious brother or priest could be found to fill an essential teaching position.

The employment of lay teachers was not an attractive proposition since it would have meant a drain on scarce financial resources at a time when there was no government assistance available either for payment of teachers, or to help with building costs and maintenance, but the practice was legitimated largely on other grounds; that they were in a class inferior to those whose commitment to teaching was part of a larger commitment to the religious way of life. The rules of the Sisters of Saint Joseph of the Most Sacred Heart of Jesus gave expression to this perspective when it mandated for its members as follows:

> When it is necessary to speak with seculars, it should be done in such a manner that people of the world may be edified and understand that they are speaking with spiritual persons, who care nothing for the vanities of the world.[10]

The notion was promoted that lay teachers could not possibly approach teaching with the same degree of responsibility as could nuns, religious brothers and priests, and also that they would ignore their duties unless they were constantly monitored. Thus, the rules of the Christian Brothers demanded that members ensure "the same conscientious discharge of duty from the lay teachers, who ought not to be allowed to bring newspapers into the classroom, much less to read them therein".[11]

Some members of religious orders were anxious that their lay counterparts would enjoy good working conditions and be happy in their schools. Even so, their approach was that of benevolent employers towards their employees rather than one informed by a view that they were partners with the lay teachers in the provision of Catholic education. This approach prevailed even in the early 1950s when it was becoming apparent that lay teachers would need to be employed in greater numbers. This view is captured well in the following extract from the minutes of the Fifth National Catholic Education Conference of Directors and Inspectors of Schools at Hobart in 1951:

> The Conference notes with dismay the alarming shortage of vocations to the religious teaching orders. Catholic lay teachers of good moral character and of sound educational qualifications can be a valuable asset, and in some cases are increasingly necessary, in Catholic schools. In this way, provision should be made for their training and financial support.[12]

It was well into the 1960s before the religious orders ceased to view lay teachers as fulfilling an essentially inferior and supplementary role.

Focusing on a definition of nuns, religious brothers and priests offers another perspective on what was distinctive about Catholic teachers who were members of religious orders. One useful definition is that they are individuals who are members of an organization dedicated to some Christian endeavor within the framework of the Catholic Church. For most of the priests, religious brothers and nuns in Australia during the period under consideration, of whom the nuns were the most visible, the endeavor in question was teaching.

Many Catholics who went to school in Australia between 1922 and 1965 have clear memories of the nuns, memories which have been shaped as much by appearance and behavior as by their sheer numbers. The Australian historian, Henderson writes of this:

> It's the nuns I remember. An oddity to outsiders, mainstream to any Catholic. Hardly a classroom was without one. They were young and in charge, and role models for the girls who looked up to them from the desks. Many of their adolescent students thought of joining them. A lot did. Some as young as sixteen. That crazy headdress gave them an exotic touch. It was called 'having a vocation'. They took vows of poverty, celibacy and obedience. They weren't part of the clergy, and they couldn't take Holy Orders like priests. But they were leaders, career women, women in the church who had a role, an alternative authority, belonging to a community

of convent life which, like their heavy clothing, separated them from everyday society.[13]

Many others have equally vivid, though less sympathetic, memories. What is of importance here, however, is that according to Canon Law, all are inaccurate when they refer to their teachers as nuns; rather, they were religious sisters.

In considering the different 'types' of female religious, Armstrong[14] has pointed out that, traditionally, Canon Law has defined nuns as belonging to an enclosed 'order' of women remaining in convents throughout their lives and devoting their time to prayer and spiritual contemplation. Religious sisters, on the other hand, take simple vows of poverty, chastity and obedience and devote themselves to 'prayer and good works'. Sturrock clarifies the matter as follows:

> The word 'Nun' is the canonical term for female religious belonging to a strictly enclosed contemplative 'Order'. The word 'Sister' is given to any religious who has taken vows and belongs to a 'Congregation'. The 'Community' to which she belongs is usually a local group and part of the wider Congregation.[15]

Magray, in a similar vein, states:

> There were two canonically valid forms of religious organization for women...First, there was the religious *order*. Women in these communities took solemn vows, were committed to strict enclosure within their convents, and received the title of *nun*. There was also a newer form of organization known as the *congregation*. Women in congregations took simple, less binding vows, worked outside the convent, and went by the title of *sister*.[16]

The popular practice in Australia throughout the period under consideration was to use both 'nuns' and 'religious orders' as generic terms and not to bother with the finer ecclesiastical distinctions in terminology, a practice which is also followed throughout most of this book.

Within most female religious orders a distinction was also made which reflected class divisions within the wider society. For many years in those European countries where the religious orders originated, only those who paid a dowry were permitted to become 'choir sisters' and train to become teachers or nurses. Those from poorer homes became 'lay sisters', wore more humble clerical garb and were restricted to domestic work within the confines of the convent. In the case of some orders, lay sisters, when attending Mass, had to remain out of view of the choir sisters in a separate section of the church. In this way, social class divisions in the general society were maintained within the convent.

A lay sister was defined as a member of a religious order who was not bound to the recitation of the Divine Office and was occupied in manual work. The separation originally arose in relation to males in Western monasticism in the Middle Ages when a distinction was made between the *oblati*, who had been placed in the monastery by their parents; and the *conversi*, who entered later in life.[17] Originally, both groups were considered to be equal but, as the abbeys became centers of learning, those who lacked the training of the *oblati*, who were illiterate, or were uneducated, came to be referred to as *conversus*. This development laid the foundation for the emergence of the same divisions within many of the female religious orders, including the teaching orders.

A significant number of the female religious orders which established themselves in Australia were originally founded amongst the growing Catholic middle class in Ireland at the end of the eighteenth and the early part of the nineteenth century, and they were particularly marked by the distinction drawn at that stage between choir sisters and lay sisters. On this, Magray has commented the following:

> Although Irish convents were primarily the stronghold of the middle class, they also attracted women of the lower classes. Typically from farming or poor urban backgrounds, these women were allowed to enter, but as 'lay' sisters who took nonbinding vows, as opposed to the choir sisters who took solemn, life-long religious vows. Such women comprised from 10 to 20 percent of the total number in a community, and they took responsibility for the domestic duties of the convent (i.e., cooking and cleaning for the rest of the sisters). Along with the elevated status that religious vows brought to these women in society at large came the understanding that they would hold an inferior status within the community.[18]

Overall, a structure developed in which lay sisters carried out the domestic work in the convents so that 'choir sisters' could be free to pray the Divine Office and engage in intellectual pursuits. The general view of the lay sisters was that they provided essential support so that the choir sisters could devote themselves fully to the apostolic work of the congregation, which was usually either teaching or nursing.

Most of the female orders introduced into Australia, whether from Ireland or Continental Europe, maintained the distinction between the two classes of nuns. This was particularly significant when it came to decision-making within the individual communities. On this, MacGinley has commented:

> All choir Sisters, even the most junior, continued to take precedence in the community over experienced and mature lay Sisters; the latter, besides some differences in their religious habits, continued in many institutes to wear aprons, a badge of servanthood, as part of their usual dress. Lay Sisters had a separate formation programme from the choir religious and a separate daily recreation period. They had no voice in chapter nor a vote in community elections. In effect two communities lived under the one roof, each impinging on the other through services and procedures regulated by ancient custom.[19]

The Sisters of Saint Joseph of the Most Sacred Heart of Jesus, founded in Australia in 1866 by Fr. Julian Tenison Woods and Mary MacKillop, were a major exception within the female teaching orders as there was only one class of membership. Indeed, a regular theme in conversations with Irish nuns who came to Australia in the 1930s, 1940s and 1950s to join this particular order was that they were attracted by its egalitarian spirit. Quite a number of them who were intellectually able had approached other orders in Ireland only to be told they would have to join as lay sisters since their backgrounds were such that they were unable to bring a dowry into the convent with them.

In the 1920s, the expressed disapproval of the Apostolic Delegate in Australia, who was the papal representative, led to the discarding of aprons by lay sisters in most religious orders. Apart from this, there was little improvement in their status until the 1950s.[20] In 1928, the Presentation Sisters in Australia, against the wishes of the Apostolic Delegate, decided to permit individual congregations to follow their existing practice which, apart from the Geraldton Congregation in Western Australia and the Longreach Congregation in Queensland, meant continuing to have lay sisters. The turning point came in 1953 when the initiative once again was taken by the Apostolic Delegate, who pointed out that Rome did not favor the distinction between choir sisters and lay sisters. The response in the various congregations, as MacGinley has stated, was that in the course of the 1950s, lay sisters were progressively absorbed into the one category of choir sisters. In most cases, she argues, "this was not achieved without some initial misgivings on both sides in view of adjustments and expectations involved".[21] By the early 1960s, however, any remaining reservations became irrelevant because the distinction between choir sisters and lay sisters was completely abolished as a result of the deliberations of the Second Vatican Council (1962–65).

Until very recently, the lay sisters were not considered by those engaged in research on the history of Catholic education in Australia.[22] To some extent, their existence remained little known even amongst the Catholic population within Australian society. By recognizing them now, it is possible to gain a greater understanding of the lives of the 'other' within the convent walls, namely, the choir sisters, who, in the case of the teaching orders, were the teachers. At the same time, it is also important to maintain a sense of balance by recalling that five out of every six of the female religious in Australia in 1950 were involved in education. Given this, and that a substantial number of the remainder were involved in other social services, it is clear that lay sisters were very much outnumbered by teaching sisters throughout the period 1922–65.[23]

Priests who conducted schools were also greatly outnumbered by teaching nuns and, to a lesser extent, by teaching brothers. These priests were members of religious orders rather than of the diocesan clergy. They had the same powers as diocesan priests in that they could celebrate Mass, remit sins, preach and administer the sacraments. However, like nuns and religious brothers, they added the vow of poverty to the vows of chastity and obedience taken by the diocesan clergy.

While very little research has been conducted on the social origins of priests in Australia, generally speaking those who were members of the diocesan clergy were from families who could afford to pay the fees charged by the diocesan seminaries. It was in these seminaries, which were under the jurisdiction of the bishops, that priests for the diocese were trained. Anyone from a less well-off background who wanted to be a priest normally joined one of the religious orders in the country which did not charge fees.

Amongst some of the religious orders of priests, including the Missionaries of the Sacred Heart, the Jesuits and the Augustinians, was the lesser rank of 'brother'. In a number of ways, these non-ordained religious brothers were the counterpart of the lay sisters, as their work consisted of domestic duties. To this was usually added heavy maintenance such as carpentry and painting, and, in some cases, farm laboring. On the mission fields, particularly in what is today Papua New Guinea, they were the real pioneers, often on the move, cutting, constructing and maintaining roads, as well as building churches, schools and houses.[24]

Religious brothers who were members of religious orders of priests differed from lay sisters in a number of ways. In certain cases, they played a significant role in the development of technical education, again particularly in the mission fields. Within Australia, they also acted in some instances rather like teacher assistants, especially through involvement in coaching school sports teams. Another way in which they differed from lay sisters was in the reason why they were allocated to the lesser ranks. This allocation had nothing to do with not having an equivalent of a choir sister's dowry on entering the order, a matter on which they were no different from priests who were members of the order. Rather, these religious brothers were individuals whose membership of the order was welcomed, but who were deemed not sufficiently highly qualified to be ordained as priests. Finally, their situation differed from the lay sisters in that they sat with the priests at meals and partook in recreation with them.

Religious brothers who were members of religious orders of priests should not be confused with those who were members of such religious orders of brothers as the Christian Brothers, the De La Salle Brothers and the Marist Brothers. Like the religious orders of nuns and priests, these religious orders of brothers also lived in a community with fellow members and took vows of poverty, chastity and obedience.

They differed from priests mainly in the fact that they were not ordained and consequently were not empowered to administer the Seven Sacraments of the Church. The great majority of them in all religious communities were involved in teaching or some form of social work. Occasionally a community also had one or two 'domestic brothers'. Again, these were individuals whose membership of the order was welcomed, but who were deemed not sufficiently highy qualified for teaching or for the other professional activities of the orders. Their principal duties were to prepare meals for the community, to keep the whole house clean, to "take care of provisions, furniture and utensils" and "to superintend farm-work or trades, and occasionally to train boys for such avocations".[25] As with lay sisters, they were seen as being important, given that they allowed their colleagues to concentrate on their professional duties, including teaching, without being distracted by domestic chores. The 'Rule' of the Christian Brothers decreed as follows :

> They [lay brothers] shall also be full of charity for the Brothers and shall serve them with joy and respect, conscious that it is Jesus Christ Whom they serve in the person of their Brothers. They shall endeavour, as far as they can, to be useful to them, to procure them what they need, and to afford them every relief, especially in sickness.[26]

At the same time, safeguards were in place to ensure that lay brothers did not become marginalized. These safeguards included the expectations that they would take their meals with the teaching brothers and join with them at recreation.

This consideration of how religious brothers and priests differed from nuns is helpful in developing further an understanding of what was distinctive about the lives of those who were teachers in Catholic schools during the period 1922–65. Considering the similarities and differences between 'lay sisters' and 'domestic brothers' is particularly useful in this regard. Yet, in the interest of balance, it should not be forgotten that the number of religious in Australia involved in education who fell into these categories was very small relative to the number who were teachers. It is with the distinctiveness of the training of these teachers that the next section of this chapter is concerned.

The Distinctiveness of the Training of Catholic Teachers

The training of nuns, religious brothers and priests who were members of religious orders often commenced with entry to a 'juniorate' at fourteen years of age. Juniorates were secondary schools which enrolled those who declared an interest in entering religious life. Depending on age and prior education, students entered an appropriate grade and usually remained until they completed their secondary schooling. While parents were sometimes asked to make a contribution to the cost of their children's education in these boarding schools, most of the costs involved were met by the religious orders who ran them.

In some ways juniorates were not very different from ordinary Catholic boarding schools, although usually the teachers were specially selected both for what was seen as their excellent teaching abilities and for their own fervent commitment to the religious way of life and to the religious order to which they belonged. There was also a somewhat greater emphasis on discipline and on saturating all aspects of life with a religious ethos. The general daily pattern was along the following lines: Students rose at about 5:45 A.M. and commenced an hour's study at 6:00 A.M. They then went to the chapel for Mass at 7:00 A.M., ate their breakfast at 8:00 A.M., and commenced a normal school day at 8:30 A.M. Lunch was at mid-day, followed by more classes. The school day finished with an hour's organized sport in the afternoon. This was followed by a set series of prayers, the rosary at 5:30 P.M. and then tea. The evening timetable consisted of study from 6:45 P.M. to 8:45 P.M., 15 minutes break, then short prayers and a hymn at 9:00 P.M., further study from 9:00 P.M. to 10:00 P.M., and then bed. Weekends were also highly organized, with timetabled study periods, interspersed with games periods, long walks and time for doing various chores, including washing clothes and polishing shoes. Once again, an emphasis on prayer was maintained, with large proportions of time being taken up with Mass in the morning, the rosary in the afternoon and religious ceremonies, including Benediction, in the chapel at night.

While standard secondary school uniforms rather than the distinctive dress of the religious orders were worn in the juniorates, this was still a first stage of initiation into the regulated way of life of the orders, particularly the organized, highly structured day of prayer and work, with little or no time for relaxing, except through partaking in sport. Girls who were in the juniorates of female religious orders generally went home on holidays twice a year and had the opportunity to meet up with relatives and old friends, even if they were expected not to go to dances. Some of the male religious orders, most notably the Christian Brothers, did not allow the boys to go home at all. For them the process of being cut off from their families commenced at a much younger age than it did for girls, although like the girls, they could write home and could also receive letters.

In the juniorate, both boys and girls got some introduction to the history and traditions of the religious orders with which they were associated. Also, while they did not engage in teaching practice, their minds were regularly oriented towards the notion of teaching as a vocation and as 'a calling from God'. Some of the orders, most notably the Sisters of Mercy and the Sisters of Saint Joseph of the Most Sacred Heart of Jesus, had juniorates in Ireland, where Irish girls enrolled with the intention of considering going to Australia to become nuns once they had finished their secondary school education. In these juniorates thousands of miles away, they formulated certain notions about the importance which the Church attached to the work of Catholic education in Australia. In particular, many found attraction in the emphasis which was placed on their possible future role in doing God's work in the education of Australian Aborigines.

Students in juniorates were regularly reminded that at the end of their secondary schooling they would have to decide whether or not to proceed to the first official stage in religious life. They were told to pray for divine enlightenment to help them make their decision, while at the same time it was emphasized that it was a grave sin not to heed 'the divine voice' which told them whether they had a 'religious vocation'. Also, while they were regularly informed that they did not have to make a commitment until the end of the juniorate years, the culture was such that, as one member of a male religious order put it, "it was not very easy to leave as there was much talk about those who had 'pulled out'. It was not considered a good thing to do".[27] Thus, the numbers of those in religious orders may have been sustained not just by a genuine commitment and by the attraction of the heroism attached to being in religious life, but also by fear of the guilt which would ensue from ignoring the divine call to serve.

Some of those who graduated from the juniorates linked with both 'ordinary' school leavers and those who had been working for a number of years, to enter the first stage of formally joining a religious order by becoming a 'postulant'. This represented a break with the past. In the case of the Christian Brothers, the period involved was only six weeks, during which the postulants continued to wear 'secular' dress. They lived with 'novices', who had progressed to the next stage and, like their female counterparts, they came under all the novitiate rules, including a decree that letters had to be handed unsealed to the superior, while mail received would be handed to the addressee with the envelope already opened.

With the Christian Brothers the six-week postulancy ended with an eight-day 'retreat' or time of intense prayer, after which the postulants became novices. The nuns, however, underwent a much longer period as postulants, usually one of eighteen months' duration. On their first day they partook in a religious ceremony at which they received a distinctive dress and neat veil. In some religious orders, most notably the Sisters of Saint Joseph of the Most Sacred Heart of Jesus, the postulants then underwent a crash course in very basic primary school teacher training for four to six weeks, including lectures on how to teach mathematics, reading and spelling. This was followed by about two months in various schools working with teachers in the classroom. Each novice was then sent out to one of a number of regional convents for twelve months and put in charge of a primary school class, with the teacher in the next classroom acting as a monitor. The novice prepared all of her own lessons, but every evening and weekend the monitor would check what she had done and how she had marked the children's books.

During this period the postulant learned to live according to the rhythms of the community. Normally she rose at 5:30 A.M. for Mass, followed by breakfast in the community dining hall, before heading off to school with some of the nuns. Here she taught until about 3:30 P.M. The next task was to clean up the classroom, sweep the floorboards, often with the help of the children and set up the chalkboard for the next day. She then had to return to the convent for community prayers at 5.00 P.M., followed by tea. After tea she sat down for what was officially 'recreation', but which was usually a time when those who were teaching marked pupils' work and prepared some lessons for the following day. This was also a time for sharing pedagogical ideas, with the more experienced nuns not only advising each other on what they found to be effective teaching methods, but also inducting the postulants into the practice of seeking their advice. This community sharing of pedagogical ideas was also a feature of the evening period set aside by the Christian Brothers for the preparation of the lessons for the following day.[28]

Postulants, then, were eased in to the life of fully professed nuns and experienced teaching and living the regulated life of a member of a religious order as intimately related. They were still not totally part of the community since they sat on their own benches at Mass and ate at their own table in the community refectory. They listened at mealtime to the spiritual writings which were read out by a community member. In this way, they learned about what was termed 'the spirit of the order', about the life of the founder or foundress, and about the heroic deeds of the early members who came to Australia and established convents, monasteries, schools and hospitals. They were also slowly molded into a state of single-mindedness, with no reading for pleasure and with an absence of the radio except insofar as it was used for teaching lessons in school. One of the few 'worldly' pleasures still available to them came from the stress which was placed on playing sport and eating plenty of what was considered to be 'good wholesome food'.[29]

As with the Christian Brothers, those who continued on beyond the postulancy became novices. The novitiate commenced with a formal reception, during which the novice was received into the religious order in the name of the Church. In the case of some orders, both the superior general and the bishop were present at this reception. It was also the occasion when full religious dress was taken on for the first time.

The novitiate usually lasted two years, although this varied somewhat from one religious order to the next. The first year, called the 'canonical year', aimed at promoting a deeper spiritual awareness in the novices. The focus was on the nature of religious life and on living according to the vows of poverty, chastity and obedience. Great emphasis was placed on coming to understand the breviary and on study of the psalms, of scripture and of theology. This took place through a combination of lectures and reading, conducted within the framework of a highly structured timetable where every minute of the day was organized and overseen by a novice master or novice mistress. These were usually very rigid individuals whose job it was to test and discern the vocation of the novices.[30] Bernstein explains the function of the novice mistress as follows:

> It was the novice mistress who trained the novices in the ways of the convent, teaching them to join their hands in a special position, to walk on the ball of the foot, to observe silence. In doing so, she was expected, if necessary, to 'break the spirit'; this was not regarded as cruelty since conformity was all.[31]

Novices were instructed in the rules of the order and were trained to accept them unquestioningly. Rules were regularly read out to them as they sat and took their daily meals in silence, although there were times when a reading of the lives of the saints was conducted instead.

This first year for the novices was viewed as a testing year to see if they could succumb to authority. They were engaged in exercises "suited to correcting defects, subduing passions, and acquiring virtues".[32] To this end, they were often given menial jobs to do, such as peeling potatoes or scrubbing floors. They also had to engage in practices which were meant to help each other reach spiritual and moral perfection. In the case of the Christian Brothers, this meant being encouraged to tell the master of novices of any misdemeanors of their peers, the argument being that this was 'to help them to help each other'. This practice was much more formalized in the case of the nuns. For the professed sisters it was called 'chapter' and was held about once a month in the chapel. Here they would prostrate themselves on the floor before the Reverend Mother and seek forgiveness for their faults. The novices had a less dramatic practice whereby they spoke to the novice mistress and related thoughts or deeds which were against the rule. This was not a substitute for the

Sacrament of Confession, but rather a relating of such transgressions as making a noise in the corridor or feeling grumpy.

Novices were also engaged in practices aimed at detaching them from possessions. For example, they had to get permission to keep gifts. If the gift was not something which was necessary in their day-to-day life they had to place it in a communal cupboard for general use. Later on, if they needed the gift and if it had not already been used by another member of the community, they had to go to the novice mistress and 'ask for small leaves', which was the term used when they sought permission to use it.

Overall, then, the first year of the novitiate was a year of spiritual preparation and of training in the religious way of life. During this year there was no mention of teaching, apart from reading the lives of well-known former members and of their work for God through the educational roles which they fulfilled. The second year, however, was very much a teacher training year. In the case of most orders, this meant primary teacher training, even for those who, at a later stage, went on to teach in secondary schools. By the 1920s all of the male religious orders involved in education had either established their own teacher training college, sent their members to one run by another order, or sent them to a state-run college or a university education department. Many of the female orders in the most populous states also had their own colleges, while in Queensland and Western Australia training continued to be provided on the earlier apprenticeship model, with some theory being imparted in classes within the convent by sisters who had done some study in the discipline of education at university.[33] MacGinley[34] has also pointed out that by the mid-1930s most of those female religious orders which judged university education to be geographically feasible ensured that at least several promising teachers availed themselves of it. At the same time, she also states that until the post-World War Two climate of expansion and improvement of educational opportunity, the total number sent to university was quite small. The practice restricted university education to a small number of intellectually gifted individuals within each order, who then had "the standing and experience to guide other teachers and to ensure good academic standards in at least the institute's leading colleges".[35]

Within the teacher training colleges run by the religious orders, novices spent some time studying the substantive content of the subjects on the state-prescribed curricula, particularly English, mathematics, history and geography. They were also introduced to psychology of education and history of education.[36] Most of the emphasis, however, was on teaching methods. They received lectures on both general teaching methods and subject-specific teaching methods. They also spent periods of time observing 'ordinary' lessons, observing lessons being taught by a 'master of method' and taking classes in Catholic schools in the local area. The 'crit' or criticism lessons were particularly feared. These were lessons which had to be given in the presence of peers and tutors, who criticized the performance in one's presence once it was over. By the 1950s the Christian Brothers had developed approaches remarkably similar to the 'micro-teaching' approaches which became very popular in state teachers' colleges in the 1970s.[37]

Throughout this teacher training year the theological and spiritual training of the novices continued, especially on weekends. They came to understand that the schools were part of the local Catholic community. Also, they learned to appreciate the extent to which parents were involved in fund-raising for the school and the manner in which they went about forming their own executives and electing their own members to the schools' parents-and-friends associations, while having no say in policy. In many cases the novices joined their trained colleagues in piling up all the desks on Friday afternoons and preparing the school so that it became the church on Sunday. Female novices, in particular, often attended Sunday Mass in the schools with the professed nuns and then stayed on in the parish to visit various families.

The end of the novitiate years led to the 'stage of first profession' to the religious way of life, the essence of which was living in the community of a religious order and leading a life of poverty, chastity and obedience. To maintain the stability of the order, commitment to this way of life is expressed publicly through the taking of vows. 'First profession' is sometimes termed 'temporary profession' and is, in a sense, a rite of passage until the final profession, which in canon law implies a perpetual commitment.[38] In the case of some religious orders this meant that vows were taken and were renewed on a yearly basis, while in the case of others it meant taking them for three years. During these periods the individual was free to reconsider his or her situation until the time of final vows, which might be anything up to nine years after the initial taking of temporary vows. All of this period was spent as an 'ordinary' member of a religious order, living the standard life of a member of the community and recognizable as a 'typical' teacher in a Catholic school.

The Authoritarian Environment in the Schools

The prevailing Catholic view on human nature during the period 1922–65 demanded an educational system which would be both highly controlled and highly controlling. In 1949 the Australian bishops summed up this view as being one which clearly rejected any 'natural goodness' thesis of human nature. Instead, what was promoted was 'the dogma of original sin'. On this, the bishops stated:

> The Catholic view is perfectly clear. Every child born into this world is a child of Adam, inheriting the nature which Adam, as it were, bequeathed to the human race. Adam's sin—the sin of direct disobedience to the command of the Almighty God—was to have disastrous effects. Evil as the results of his sin were, however, they did not completely corrupt human nature. They disfigured it—but not beyond hope of repair.[39]

Thus, the task of education was "to restore the sons of Adam to their high position as children of God, citizens of the kingdom of God, by the harmonious development of their physical, social, intellectual, moral, aesthetic and spiritual powers".[40] Both the home and the school, as Praetz points out, were seen as having a central role to play in this process:

> At home, children must be loved but also trained in co-operative habits, definitely formed by the time the child comes to school. Schools inculcated moral virtues, fortifying the will through the exclusion of negative influences and strengthening motives for good conduct through positive training and instruction.[41]

While such a view demanded that schools exercise a very great deal of control over pupils, it did not necessarily preclude the promotion of intellectualism or the adoption of humanitarian approaches in teacher-pupil relationships. Officially the Church was not opposed to a consideration of alternative views to its position on a variety of issues; rather, what was important was that the fundamental faults within such alternative views, as the Church saw them, be exposed and debated, thus leading to 'informed convictions' rather than 'blind faith'. This, after all, was the basis of the Jesuit's Ratio Studiorum, a pedagogical approach emphasizing mental training in logical argument.[42] Similarly, the Franciscan tradition emphasized gentleness and the beholding of the beauty of God in nature, while much of Ursuline pedagogical theory is based on the notion that education should be structured so that it is the child's intrinsic interest in learning which is promoted.[43]

What operated within Australian Catholic schools bore little of the hallmarks of some of these older pedagogical traditions within the Church. Instead, what eventuated was a set of practices which reflected the authoritarian nature of the rules and regulations of the dominant religious orders involved in education, and an intersection between these rules and the social conditions of the Australian Catholic population. In particular, the training of those in religious orders to live within an authoritarian framework meant that they operated their schools within similar parameters. In other words, their life, which was highly organized around a uniform program and an inflexible rule that regulated every detail of daily living under a strict internal government, was replicated in the schools. In this way, the school environment presented no threat to the habitual ways in which teachers who were members of religious orders had been trained to think and act.

A variety of classroom practices emanating from the authoritarian nature of the rules governing religious life were viewed as being of benefit to pupils later on in life. The emphasis which teachers who were members of religious orders placed on being highly organized, on attending carefully to the preparation of schoolwork, and on ensuring that schoolrooms were models of neatness and tidiness, all prepared pupils to become obedient employees. The spiritual training received by nuns, religious brothers and priests also equipped them for developing a capacity for hard work in their students. This applied not just to mental work, but also to physical work. Indeed, the teachers led by example. They did much of the school maintenance themselves and, at times, if money was not available, they also did the school cleaning. They regularly involved their students in this work, especially at weekends and in the first few days of the school vacation periods. The religious orders justified such activity not only as being necessary because of the reluctance on the part of the state to provide financial support for Catholic education, but also on the grounds that hard work and even a certain amount of physical suffering is necessary for salvation.

The stress within Catholicism on accepting the Church's definition of a situation and following its rules and regulations as a means of salvation is also significant. On this, the religious orders went to the extreme in their programs of spiritual preparation for their members by producing personalities who would not question their rules.[44] Thus, critical debate was actively discouraged. This, in turn, was reflected in school policy and practice. The outcome in the case of Christian Brothers' schools was, as Angus has put it, a 'no frills' curriculum, that guided pupils towards achieving success in state examinations, but with an emphasis on "marks rather than understanding".[45] In other words, rote learning was promoted and intellectual concerns were "reduced to a functional, mechanistic production of credentials".[46]

While Angus is correct in attributing this approach to the historical mission of the Christian Brothers in educating Catholic boys for social and career advancement, the anti-intellectualism enshrined within the rules of the order cannot be overlooked. For example, it was made clear to Christian Brothers during their period of spiritual training that while they should be taught to avoid "a slothful culpable indifference which causes them to neglect study", they should also avoid "an inordinate love of study which may injure piety and health".[47] The situation was clarified as follows:

> There are certain dangers attending study which can and must be guarded against. *Knowledge puffeth up*, and unless counterbalanced by humility,

leads to destruction. Plausible excuses often betray the earnest student to indulge in light literature; the necessity for a good style and richness of thought are special baits. If such reading leads to the loss of devotion, what a price has been paid for an unnecessary advantage. Study in itself is not a spiritual work and, even when innocently pursued, tends to dry up the soul. When pursued too eagerly it often leads to a restless desire for it, when duty requires one's whole attention to other things; under such circumstances, it leads to unpunctuality, to studying at wrong times, to preoccupying one's thoughts during prayer, and often, alas, to the neglect of Spiritual Exercises.[48]

Thus, every Christian Brother was forbidden to read books or publications other than those in the community library, had to have the special consent of his superior for any reading not connected with his studies, and was not allowed to "study or read secular books in his cell without permission".[49] In similar vein, the mistress of novices in the Brigidine Order in Victoria during much of the period under consideration summarized her expectations of those who wished to join the order as follows:

Brilliance, talent, genius are not necessary; in fact they are if anything undesirable for success in community life except with an Aquinian grace of humility, but a genius for taking pains, character, patience, industry and virtue are, on the contrary, essential.[50]

Given this perspective, it is not surprising that teachers who were members of religious orders were not, in turn, inclined to encourage the development of a questioning approach amongst pupils.

Here one might be inclined to suggest that the pedagogical practices and general educational approach of a number of other religious orders were more enlightened. In this regard, orders like the Jesuit Fathers, the Loreto Sisters and the sisters of the Religious of the Sacred Heart certainly adopted a more intellectual approach while also introducing students to a broad range of 'high culture' experiences and 'social graces'. However, not only did these orders concentrate on educating those in the upper levels of Catholic society, but their own membership was very small in comparison with the membership of the dominant orders.

What is being suggested here, then, is that the majority of the teaching force in Catholic schools viewed teaching as a set of technical activities to be executed in an inflexible manner, rather than as a repertoire of intelligent practices to be varied according to unique classroom contexts. This is not to overlook the imaginative ways in which Catholic teachers coped with very large classes and scarce resources.[51] Neither is it to ignore those rules of the various orders which stated that members should "carefully study methods of teaching, the most effective means of reaching the understanding of the pupils and of communicating knowledge to them".[52] Rather, it is to recognize that even when they embraced progressive pedagogical practices, Catholic teachers were not encouraged to contemplate the epistemological foundations of these practices; something, of course, which is not surprising given that such relativist foundations were often diametrically opposed to the certitude of Catholic doctrine.[53]

The rules of the religious orders also operated to subdue any notion that education might be about fostering interpersonal relationships between teachers and pupils. The consequences of this were not all negative. The rules insisted that no pupils should be favored over others and that teachers should never allow themselves to be alone with pupils. This, in turn, was related to the rule that personal friendships were not to develop between the members of the religious orders; even when it came to recreation, they were expected to walk in threes rather than in twos, as anything bordering on 'particular friendships' was frowned upon, particularly since it might be seen as a sign of homosexual tendencies.[54]

Such rules appear to have grown out of the notion that spirituality could only be built up by laying aside one's sensitivity and need for love and affection, although they were also seen to be necessary to ensure fidelity to the vow of chastity. The implication for the classroom, however, was that any emphasis on education as a reciprocal encounter in which teacher and pupil aspired towards the closeness of interpersonal dialogue, was ruled out. In short, teachers were brought to view themselves as directive, controlling and task-oriented individuals as opposed to being concerned with the development of feelings and emotions. On this, the 'Rule' of the Christian Brothers took a very negative view of human nature when instructing the master of novices to take the following approach with his charges:

> The indolent must be urged forward and employed at hard work; they
> should not be left idle at any time, nor allowed to assume a negligent
> posture when sitting, standing, or kneeling, or even a posture that is very
> comfortable; they should be obliged to do perfectly and promptly what
> they are told to do; they should understand that the religious life is a life
> of labour and devoutness.[55]

Similarly, the mistress of novices in the Sisters of Mercy was
instructed to ensure that those under her tutelage were to be taught
"modesty, meekness and humility" and were to be encouraged to
"conquer those pettish and childish honors which weaken the spirit".[56]
The consequence for education was that teachers who had undertaken
a program of 'spiritual formation' based upon such views created a
regimen within their classrooms which modeled that of the novitiate,
thus ensuring that day-dreaming, frivolity and the allocation of time
for activity to be undertaken at a relaxed pace were discouraged lest
'the Devil find work for idle hands'.

The program of 'spiritual formation' for nuns, religious brothers
and priests who were teachers also resulted in a variety of practices
within the schools which were certainly not in accordance with any
official pedagogical position of the religious orders to which they
belonged. For example, the humiliation to which some female pupils
were subjected by nuns in the presence of their peers can be seen as
mirroring the experience which those same teachers had at the hands
of their Mistress of Novices, who operated under instructions of the
following type:

> The proud and pretentious must be humbled by occasionally assigning to
> them the meanest employments, by their being made to feel that pride is
> altogether opposed to the spirit of Jesus Christ, that this vice is the root of
> all evils, that it vitiates the best actions, that God despises the proud, that
> sooner or later He humbles them, and that even their fellow-men cannot
> bear them.[57]

There was never any intention that teachers should, in turn, adopt
such a rule in their own dealings with their pupils. Nevertheless, some
did. This situation can be attributed either to a failure on the part
of the teachers to distinguish between their own 'spiritual formation'
as members of a religious order and what was appropriate

in the classroom, or to inflicting on pupils the frustration and humiliation which they themselves experienced within the cloister. Similarly, it became a practice in many girls' boarding schools for teachers to read pupils' mail before it was sent or received. This was not part of any official requirement. Rather, it mirrored the relationship which existed between the nuns and their religious superiors when it came to personal correspondence. Again, it is possible to view such action by nuns towards pupils as an unreflective modeling of the behavior of the mistress of novices. At the most extreme, the action may have been motivated by bitterness on the part of those who resented similar intrusion by their superiors into their own privacy.

The notion that bitterness was generated within some teachers in response to various experiences to get them to learn how to aim for 'perfection' by "dying to themselves and the world"[58] also goes some way towards explaining the excessive use of corporal punishment by some of the male teaching orders. The Christian Brothers have the most "unenviable reputation"[59] in this regard. Their image has been characterized as one of teachers who were "quite unusually and exceptionally severe, more unrestrained than teachers in general, more uncontrolled than members of other Religious Institutes serving the Catholic people".[60] The fact that, unlike those who became priests or nuns, most of those who became Christian Brothers were recruited in their early teens, was probably a significant factor in the aggressive disposition adopted by some. What is being suggested here is that the 'normal' turmoil of early to middle adolescent years is unsettling enough psychologically, without having to subdue desires and passions to come to be able to live within the extraordinary authoritarian framework of the consecrated celibate life. The associated repression for some became manifest in various ways, one of which was the very high level of physical punishment of pupils, especially when faced with enormous numbers in class.

By the late 1950s change was on the horizon. As many migrants settled, the need for new Catholic parishes grew in areas with little or no infrastructure. The attitude of the Australian church required school places for every Catholic child, so no limit was placed on enrolments, with class sizes growing as a result. Indeed, classes of sixty and seventy pupils were reported by Melbourne inspectors during the 1960s. The situation was compounded when, in the late 1960s and early 1970s, the number of people entering religious orders decreased.

The inability of religious congregations to meet the increased demand for teaching staff meant that recruitment and employment of lay teachers, largely trained in government institutions, became the only real alternative. The change in the mixture of staff led to the appointment of lay principals and the withdrawal of religious congregations from individual schools. Catholic schools were now returning to the pattern of the earlier part of the nineteenth century of lay teachers dominating the teaching force. These, of course, were teachers who had not been through the lengthy period of spiritual formation of those they replaced. This development, as the next chapter points out, also coincided with a move away from the dogmatic approach to the teaching of religion which was prevalent during the period 1922–65. Accordingly, the authoritarian framework which had characterized schools during the years when they were dominated by the religious orders was no longer seen as quite so essential to the Church in its primary mission in the schools.

Notes

[1] W. F. Connell, *Reshaping Australian Education: 1960–1985* (Hawthorn, Victoria, Australia: Australian Council for Educational Research, 1993), p. 132.

[2] R. Fogarty, *Catholic Education in Australia 1806–1950* (Melbourne: Melbourne University Press, 1959), p. 388.

[3] The Christian Brothers, *Directory and Rules of the Congregation of the Brothers of the Christian Schools of Ireland* (Dublin: The Christian Brothers, 1927), p. 258. In the case of many of the female religious orders the emphasis on 'quitting the world' meant that a nun could not even visit a dying relative or attend a parent's funeral without special permission, which was rarely given. See, for example, Sisters of Saint Joseph of the Most Sacred Heart of Jesus, *Customs and Practices of the Sisters of St. Joseph of the Most Sacred Heart of Jesus* (Sydney: Sisters of Saint Joseph of the Most Sacred Heart of Jesus, 1950), pp. 14–15.

[4] The Sisters of Mercy, *Constitutions of the Congregation of the Australian Union of the Sisters of Our Lady of Mercy* (Canberra, Australia: The Sisters of Mercy—General Motherhouse, 1960), p. 2.

[5] The Christian Brothers, *Directory and Rules of the Congregation of the Brothers of the Christian Schools of Ireland*, p. 258.

[6] The Institute of the Blessed Virgin Mary, *Rules IBVM* (Dublin: IBVM, 1914), p. 27.

[7] The Sisters of Mercy, *A Guide for the Religious Called Sisters of Mercy* (London: Robson and Son, 1866), p. 97.

[8] The Presentation Sisters, *Constitutions of the Presentation Sisters* (Cork, Ireland: Hickey and Byrne, 1928), p. 27.

[9] The Christian Brothers, *Directory and Rules of the Congregation of the Brothers of the Christian Schools of Ireland*, p. 169.

[10] Sisters of Saint Joseph of the Most Sacred Heart of Jesus, *Customs and Practices of the Sisters of St. Joseph of the Most Sacred Heart of Jesus*, p. 7.

[11] The Christian Brothers, *Directory and Rules of the Congregation of the Brothers of the Christian Schools of Ireland*, p. 169.

[12] See file entitled 'General Educational Matters'. Box 29. File 5. Archdiocese of Perth Archives. Perth, Australia.

[13] A. Henderson, *Mary MacKillop's Sisters: A Life Unveiled* (Sydney: Harper-Collins Publishers, 1997), p. 1.

[14] K. Armstrong, *Through the Narrow Gate* (London: Pan Books Ltd., 1982), pp. 68–69.

[15] M. Sturrock, *Women of Strength, Women of Gentleness—Brigidine Sisters, Victoria Province* (Melbourne: David Lovell Publishing, 1995), p. xi.

[16] M. P. Magray, *The Transforming Power of the Nuns* (New York: Oxford University Press, 1998), p. 138, n. 14.

[17] *New Catholic Encyclopedia, Vol. 8* (New York: McGraw-Hill, 1967), p.575.

[18] M. P. Magray, *The Transforming Power of the Nuns*, p. 42.

[19] M. R. MacGinley, *A Dynamic of Hope: Institutes of Women Religious in Australia* (Sydney: Crossing Press, 1996), p. 320.

[20] Ibid.

[21] Ibid.

[22] See, for example, C. Trimingham-Jack, 'The lay sister in educational history and memory', Proceedings of the ANZHES Annual Conference, Auckland, New Zealand, 1998.

[23] A consideration of the situation in Western Australia can help to illustrate the general pattern in more detail:

Table 3.1: Comparison for Western Australia (WA)
Between the Total No. of Nuns and the Total No. Teaching

Year	Total No. of Nuns in WA	Total No. of Nuns Teaching in WA
1940	1051	910
1960	1454	1052

Source: *The Australasian Catholic Record* for the years in question.

The following table facilitate a comparison to be made between the number of nuns in Western Australia who were teaching and those involved in other areas of activity:

Table 3.2: No. of Nuns in Western Australia: 1940–60

Congregations Involved Primarily in Education	1940	1950	1960
Mercy Sisters	343	329	378
Presentation Sisters	109	111	137
St. Joseph of the Sacred Heart	84	87	108
Our Lady of the Apparition	58	100	111
Our Lady of the Missions	86	96	99
Dominican Sisters	51	62	77
Loreto Sisters	41	41	41
Oblate Benedictines	9	12	21
Brigidine Sisters		14	18
Ursuline Sisters			10
Schoenstaat Sisters		12	

Congregations Involved Primarily in Areas Other Than Education	1940	1950	1960
St. John of God Sisters	245	236	278
Little Sisters of the Poor	15	23	20
Poor Sisters of Nazareth	4	8	14
Good Shepherd Sisters		25	23
Poor Sisters of Our Lady		17	
Sisters of Holy Family of Nazareth			5
Daughters of Charity			6

Source: *The Australasian Catholic Record* for the years in question.

At the same time, however, it can be seen that the membership of nearly all of the congregations not primarily involved in education was very small. The one exception was the St. John of God Sisters, whose main work was in health care. Numerically, their involvement in education was very small, being confined to mission work in the Kimberley region, in the northwest of the state. The Sisters of Mercy also extended their work beyond schooling to include nursing and social work. Indeed, all of the congregations of religious sisters involved in education in Western Australia were involved to various degrees in other activities, particularly nursing, the care of the aged, and social work.

24   I have dealt with this to some extent in T. A. O'Donoghue, 'The Sacred Heart Mission and education in Papua 1885–1942', *Journal of Educational Administration and History*, Vol. 25, No. 1, 1993, pp. 58–71.

25   The Christian Brothers, *Directory and Rules of the Congregation of the Brothers of the Christian Schools of Ireland*, p. 278.

26   Ibid.

27   This is a common theme in the interviews conducted with religious brothers as part of the project on which this book is based.

28   This is another common theme in interviews conducted with Christian Brothers.

29   This is a common theme in the interviews conducted with nuns as part of the project on which this book is based.

30 See M. B. Bernstein, *Nuns* (Glasgow: Collins, 1978), p. 83.

31 Ibid.

32 Ibid.

33 M. R. MacGinley, *A Dynamic of Hope: Institutes of Women Religious in Australia* (Sydney: Crossing Press, 1996), p. 280.

34 Ibid., p. 281

35 Ibid., p. 282.

36 Ibid.

37 This is a common theme in the interviews conducted with Christian Brothers as part of the project on which this book is based. See also T. A. Simpson, 'A historical review of microteaching' (unpublished M.A. thesis, Macquarie University, 1987).

38 See M. B. Bernstein, *Nuns*, p. 87.

39 Episcopal Committee for Catholic Action, Social Justice Statement, *Christian Education in a Democratic Community* (Carnegie, Victoria, Australia: Renown, 1949), p. 4.

40 Ibid.

41 H. Praetz, *Building a School System: A Sociological Study of Catholic Education* (Melbourne: Melbourne University Press, 1980), p. 19.

42 See A. S. Bryk, V. E. Lee and P. B. Holland, *Catholic Schools and the Common Good* (Cambridge: Harvard University Press, 1993), p. 31.

43 See P. M. Waters, *The Ursuline Achievement: A Philosophy of Education for Women* (North Carlton, Australia: Colonna, 1994).

44 See Sisters of St. Joseph of the Most Sacred Heart of Jesus, *Customs and Practices of the Sisters of St. Joseph of the Most Sacred Heart of Jesus*, p. 4. Here it is stated that sisters "should love and honour their Superiors as those who are in the place of Christ and show this love on all occasions. They must speak to them with reverence, and when the Superior speaks should listen to her without interrupting, and take her commands, advice, or correction with humility, without excusing themselves". See also The Sisters of the Brigidine Congregation, *The Constitutions of the Sisters of the Brigidine Congregation* (New South Wales, Australia: The Sisters of the Brigidine Congregation, 1956), p. 19. Here the following requirement is laid down: "The Novices when they receive reproof or advice from their Mistress, shall listen to her in a spirit of utmost faith and submission. Being fully persuaded that their Superiors seek only to form them to virtue, they will receive with humility and gratitude the admonitions and corrections given to them".

45 L. Angus, 'Class, culture and curriculum: A study of continuity and change in a Catholic school, in R. Bates, L. Smith, L. Angus and P. Watkins (eds.), *Continuity and Change in Catholic Education: An Ethnography of Christian Brothers College* (Victoria, Australia: Deakin University, 1982), p. 60.

46 Ibid.

47 The Christian Brothers, *Directory and Rules of the Congregation of the Brothers of the Christian Schools of Ireland*, p. 287.

48 Ibid.

49 Ibid., p. 284.

[50] M. Sturrock, *Women of Strength, Women of Gentleness—Brigidine Sisters, Victoria Province*, p. 64.

[51] For some government inspectors' reports on this see the archives of the Archdiocese of Perth, *Report of the Government Inspector on St. Francis Xavier Primary School, Armadale*, 17 June 1942. Here the use of project books in geography is noted, as is the "acting out of poems representing characters" and "dramatization in social studies". Again, the *Report of the Government Inspector on Bedford Park Primary School*, 25 September 1944 noted as follows: "It was very pleasing to see the many activities connected with various subjects; among these, debates, lecturettes, manual work, art, verse speaking, charts and research work were of outstanding merit".

[52] The Christian Brothers, *Directory and Rules of the Congregation of the Brothers of the Christian Schools of Ireland*, p. 286.

[53] See H. Praetz, *Building a School System: A Sociological Study of Catholic Education*, p. 19.

[54] I have elaborated on this in T. A. O'Donoghue, *The Catholic Church and the Secondary School Curriculum in Ireland, 1922–1962* (New York: Peter Lang Publishing, 1999), p. 52.

[55] The Christian Brothers, *Directory and Rules of the Congregation of the Brothers of the Christian Schools of Ireland*, p. 357.

[56] The Sisters of Mercy, *Constitutions of the Congregation of the Australian Union of the Sisters of Our Lady of Mercy*, p. 115.

[57] Ibid.

[58] Ibid.

[59] B. Coldrey, 'A most unenviable reputation: The Christian Brothers and school discipline over two centuries', *History of Education*, Vol. 21, No. 3, 1992, pp. 277–289.

[60] Ibid., p. 277.

Chapter Four

Religion in the Schools

The previous chapter demonstrated that teaching in Catholic schools in Australia during the period 1922–65 was both overseen and conducted by a teaching force made up almost entirely of individuals who were members of religious orders and who had experienced an intensive program of 'religious formation'. The chapter focused in particular on the authoritarian framework within which the 'formation' took place, adopting the position that such a framework influenced all aspects of the lives of the religious, including their work as teachers. This position is now developed further by examining the emphasis which was placed on religion in the schools. The nature and extent of the emphasis was a result of the expectation of the Catholic Church internationally that its schools would play a central part in creating within students a belief in, and adherence to, its teachings. It was an expectation which manifested itself in three major ways: through the formal teaching of religion classes, through the stress placed on infusing the 'secular' subjects with religious content, and through a range of practices which ensured that Catholic schools had an all-pervasive religious atmosphere.

The Teaching of Religion

So serious was the Church in its insistence that Catholic schools would play a central part in creating within students a belief in, and adherence to, its teachings, that priests in certain dioceses were strongly urged by their superiors to build a school first before building a presbytery or a church. State schools were not acceptable, being seen as a source of great evil. This view underpinned the instruction to the mistresses of novices of the Sisters of Saint Joseph of the Most Sacred Heart of Jesus that they should impress upon novices the need "to prepare themselves for the great work of rescuing souls from the almost certain destruction which awaits them in the secular schools of the age".[1] Non-Catholic children were occasionally admitted to a Catholic school, but the Church decreed that every precaution had to be taken to safeguard the faith of the Catholic children in such circumstances. No non-Catholic minister was ever to be admitted to Catholic schools to give religious instruction and non-Catholic children were to be enrolled only on condition that they attended prayers, catechism lessons and other devotions with Catholic children. By contrast, Catholic priests were usually at liberty to enter a government school and give instruction at certain allotted times to any Catholic children who were enrolled.

Competence in the teaching of religion was the principal justification for the domination of the Catholic teaching force by religious.[2] As the *Directory of the Brigidine Sisters* put it:

> It is a duty incumbent on the Sisters to teach the children Christian Doctrine, for which they must qualify themselves. They shall accustom them to think and speak reverently to God and of holy things, and not allow them to be over-curious in their questions; but constantly exhort them to captivate their understanding in obedience to Faith; and to keep their minds always disposed to receive instruction from those whom Christ has appointed to rule His Church.[3]

In similar vein, the Sisters of Saint Joseph of the Most Sacred Heart of Jesus decreed that "religious instruction must be the Sisters' first care, otherwise the object of our schools is defeated".[4] Therefore, Catholic schools were organized so that space was allocated on their timetables for religion classes. Various titles were assigned to these classes at different times and in different places. They included 'religious instruction', 'catechetics', 'religious education' and 'Christian doctrine'. Each year the pupils in Catholic primary schools in every diocese had an oral examination in 'religion' conducted by a representative of the local bishop, while pupils in Catholic secondary schools had both an oral and a written examination.

Flynn's three-stage linear model of 'traditional catechesis', 'kerygmatic catechesis' and 'experiential catechesis' is useful for developing an account of the changes which took place in the teaching of religion in Australian Catholic schools during the period 1922–65.[5] 'Traditional catechesis' emerged around the time of the Council of Trent (1545–63) and led to the development of the 'catechism'.[6] The Church's view was that it had been provided with a body of truth and that the most suitable way to pass it on to its members was through the catechism. This new approach replaced earlier forms of oral instruction as the prime source of Catholic teaching.

In the early 1800s catechisms consisted of a methodical summary of the teachings of the Church, with the emphasis being moralistic and doctrinal. By the middle of the century Australian Catholic schools were using a variety of catechisms prepared and authorized by the country's bishops, the most common one being popularly known as the 'Penny Catechism'.[7] Such catechisms were usually small concise books with a list of several hundred short questions and accompanying prepared answers. Students were required to commit the answers to memory and to recite them orally when requested to do so. The questions were laid out on the following lines:

Who made the world?

God made the world.

Who is God?

God is the Creator of heaven and earth and of all things and the supreme Lord of all.

Campion has argued that such "directness and sureness", as well as the simplicity of the prose used, "imparted a special brand of confidence". By way of illustration, he quotes the following summation of "a great theological truth":

Why did God make us?

God made us to know, love and serve Him here on earth; and
to see and enjoy Him forever in heaven.

Yet Campion has also contended that the catechism could be
deceptive, that at times "it must have puzzled and perhaps stretched
the minds of the young learners"[8] with entries like the following:

Which are the principal mysteries of religion?
There are two principal mysteries of religion:
First, the Unity and Trinity of God; Secondly, the Incarnation,
Death and Resurrection of Our Saviour.

The point is that such sophisticated concepts were dealt with in
primary schools solely through learning by rote and committing
to memory without discussion or explanation.

One nun who used catechisms in the Diocese of Sandhurst in the
late 1940s has reminisced as follows: "As far back as I can remember,
we had half an hour the first thing in the morning, during which we
said the morning prayers and then we drilled in the catechism".[9]
When, in 1958, teachers in the Archdiocese of Melbourne were
canvassed on the effects of this practice of 'drilling in the catechism'
on pupils' attitudes to religion, they expressed dissatisfaction. Yet, as
Praetz has pointed out, they also showed no willingness to change
their practices because, as a synopsis of faith, "the catechism had
formed part of the religious training of the teachers both at school
and at the novitiate" and "its use simplified the work of teachers and
inspectors".[10] In other words, it was a teaching control device as well
as a device for the teaching of religion.

The drilling method aimed at committing text to memory was
not, of course, unique to the teaching of religion. Equally, even
though it held the pre-eminent position, the catechism was not the
only means of teaching religion. On this, the same nun mentioned
above also remembered another daily lesson: "The last half an hour
before lunch time was more devotional, like there would be probably
bible stories. On Fridays we would teach something about the Mass and
we'd also tell stories about the lives of the saints".[11]

Various syllabi were prepared to guide teachers as to how religion was to be taught. For example, the *Syllabus of Religious Instruction in Schools* prepared for the Melbourne Archdiocese, was issued in separate editions in 1917 and 1933. In 1950, a similar document was prepared for distribution to all Catholic schools in Victoria.[12] This latter syllabus covered schooling 'from kindergarten to matriculation' and provided notes on suggested timetables, on how to manage a number of classes of several grade levels simultaneously, and on how to organize student projects. It then dealt with each grade level individually, providing short specific instructions under various headings. The headings used in the kindergarten section were 'Suggested Bible Stories', 'Moral Instructions', 'Prayers', 'Form of Morning Prayers Used in the Kindergarten', 'Aspirations', 'Hymns', 'Pictures to be Used', and 'Dramatization'. By grade six these headings were extended to include 'Doctrine', 'Catechism', 'Sacred Scripture', 'Projects', 'Apparatus', and 'Term Tests'. For the final years of secondary schooling details on specific aspects of 'Church History', 'Liturgy' and 'Social Doctrine' were included.

The only students encouraged to examine the Church's teachings were those amongst the relatively small number who progressed to the senior levels in secondary school and studied 'apologetics'. This approach was designed to help them defend their faith through systematic argumentation, "demonstrating the truth of such beliefs as the existence of God, the divinity of Jesus, the Catholic Church as the one true church, and the infallibility of the Pope".[13] Some schools also placed an emphasis on the teaching of Catholic social philosophy at this level. The origins of such philosophy are to be found in the Catholic social movement which began on the continent of Europe in the late nineteenth century and whose ideas were worked out by continental theologians.[14] These ideas were summed up and ratified by Pope Leo XII when he issued his encyclical, *Rerum Novarum*, in 1891, which left a wide range of social and economic policies open to Catholics while ruling out some extreme courses: "As against socialism, it asserted man's right to private property. As against individualism, it asserted the State's right to intervene against bad working conditions".[15] What was proposed was an ideal of class harmony towards which Christians should aim. This ideal was reiterated in Pope Pius XI's encyclical of 15 May 1931, *Quadragesimo Anno*.[16] Here it was proposed that the members of each industry or profession be organized in 'vocational groups' or 'corporations' in which employers and workers would collaborate in furthering their common interests. To do so, it was argued, would be to act in accordance with the basic principle of Catholic social philosophy, the 'principle of subsidiary function'.[17] The essence of this principle was summarized as follows: "It is an injustice and at the same time a grave evil and disturbance of higher order to assign to a greater and higher association what lesser and subordinate organisations can do".[18]

The 'principle of subsidiary function' developed out of a commitment to maintaining and promoting the dignity of the human person at a time when many were caught between the anarchy of traditional capitalism and the totalitarianisms of right and left. It also gave Catholics in Australia another rationale and justification for the existence of their separate educational sector. Furthermore, it resulted in schools being encouraged to teach pupils "through discussion and instruction", the "principles of the great social encyclicals on anti-capitalism and communism".[19] One outcome of such encouragement was the inclusion in 1950 of texts on 'Social Doctrine' on the religion syllabus for final year secondary school students in Victoria.[20] Yet, the majority of Catholics were not exposed to such texts since they did not progress to secondary school. For them, the experience of religious education was largely one of learning prayers, committing to memory dogma imparted in an unquestioning manner, and listening to, and reading about the 'story' of the Church, beginning with the early Christian times.

Some work aimed at improving the quality of religious education was undertaken by a number of Catholic educationalists in Australia. While accepting the broad parameters of what was prescribed for the teaching of religion in both primary and secondary schools, these individuals argued that much of what was being imparted was not meaningful to pupils because of the nature of the technical language and theological terminology Amongst those who set out to produce more 'pupil-friendly' textbooks in the 1920s and 1930s were Fr. A. E. O'Brien of the Diocese of Bathurst, and Archbishop Michael Sheehan,

Brother Hanrahan and Fr. T. J. O'Connor, all of the Archdiocese of Sydney.[21] A group of priests under the direction of Dr. Beovich, Archbishop of Adelaide, responded along similar lines in a new catechism produced in 1938 and used in Victoria, South Australia, parts of Tasmania and some of the dioceses of New South Wales.[22]

Fr. John McMahon, who held the post of Director of Education in the Archdiocese of Perth, was one of the most innovative figures in religious education in Australia at the time. He had undertaken significant research on the teaching of religion both at University College Dublin and at the Catholic University of America in Washington D.C. He produced a series of textbooks for the teaching of religion in the schools of Western Australia, employing methods of instruction based on the parable style of teaching exemplified in the Gospels. In his advice to teachers, McMahon anticipated many pedagogical ideas which did not come to prominence amongst the general educational community until the middle to late 1960s.[23] His advocacy that teaching should involve constantly returning, and at increasing levels of sophistication, to a series of central concepts,[24] mirrored some of the ideas later encompassed in Bruner's notion of 'the spiral curriculum'.[25] Another idea he promoted which was echoed in Bruner's work was that learning should be based not only on the imparting of propositional knowledge, but should also involve 'doing' and 'acting out'. Finally, McMahon explicitly emphasized 'reflective practice', arguing that teachers should regularly 'capture reflections during teaching', often on a sheet of paper, so that they could then be considered later on in the day for their potential to improve practice.[26]

McMahon's ideas found expression in his program of religious education initiated in the 1930s for remote regions of Western Australia. Popularly known as the 'bushies' scheme', it started with vacation courses in religious education for rural children provided in various urban centers to give the necessary foundation for correspondence courses provided later in their homes.[27] The scheme began in a rented dwelling in Perth where rural children were accommodated for several weeks each year to attend religion classes conducted on a voluntary basis by nuns, religious brothers and priests. It was subsequently expanded into a network of 'religious holiday schools' in towns throughout Western Australia. These schools were attended by children from outlying regions for two or three weeks every year. The children were boarded in convents or with Catholic families, given intensive courses in religious education in the schools, provided with textbooks and assigned a teacher with whom they could correspond when they returned home. All costs were covered by funds raised by volunteers. In the late 1950s the scheme was extended by the addition of 'motor-missions'. The Sisters of Saint Joseph of the Most Sacred Heart of Jesus started the first motor-mission in 1959 to serve the southeast wheatbelt area, and in 1964 the Sisters of Our Lady of the Missions operated a motor-mission to serve the Narrogin-Ravensthorpe area. The sisters traveled by car and gave religious instruction through a network of government schools in each district and, in addition, visited and worked with parents and family groups.

The developments in Western Australia provided the model for similar developments throughout Australia and New Zealand for the religious instruction of children from isolated areas, many of which had neither churches nor schools. Fogarty has described the progress as follows:

> In Melbourne, as a result of the mission section of the National Eucharistic Congress held in that city in 1934, the National Correspondence Course was launched under the direction of the Reverend Dr. James Hannan. The first lessons were despatched in the middle of the next year to 7,000 children in the diocese of Melbourne, Sandhurst, Ballarat, Sale and Goulburn. By the end of that year 14,000 children were enrolled, the scheme having been extended to the diocese of Port Augusta, Adelaide, Hobart, and Toowoomba. Later the dioceses of Rockhampton, Lismore, and Darwin joined in. Most of the New South Wales dioceses entered another scheme inaugurated in Sydney in 1936. Later still the dioceses of Adelaide, Maitland and Hobart set up their own.[28]

Such developments, while adventurous and responsive to local situations, were reflective of the 'traditional approach' to teaching religion, being focused on the transmission of a specific body of knowledge and practices. Yet new ideas were beginning to break through. While the debate generated coincided approximately with the Second Vatican Council (1962–65), the ideas themselves originated much earlier. Some suggest they went back to the work of the German

Jesuit theologian, Josef Jungmann, in the 1930s. He was concerned that the Church's emphasis on doctrine and formulae had made these things 'ends in themselves'.[29]

Jungmann's central notion was that the focus should be on the essential message of Christian teaching, the *kerygma*; hence the name 'kerygmatic catechesis'. As he saw it, the conveyance of knowledge was not as important as an examination of the central basis of 'the Faith'. He emphasized that Christianity should be seen not just as a system of truths or a code of rules, but as a message, the 'good news'. Thus, it was argued, catechetics should be personalized, following the behavior of human intercourse, and be 'christocentric', that is, moulding all its elements around the central figure of Christ.

In Australia, the emphasis on the kerygmatic approach resulted in the appearance, with general episcopal approval, of several new texts between 1962 and 1964.[30] They were prepared by a team led by a priest of the Melbourne Catholic Education Office, Fr. John Kelly, and were based on a German catechism of 1949. The noticeable feature of Kelly's texts was their dependence on the Bible. In the accompanying teachers' book the pedagogical methods used by Jesus were recommended.[31]

Kelly's works were very much in line with Vatican thinking, particularly the position expounded in 1965 in the Second Vatican Council's *Gravissimum Educationis* (*Declaration on Christian Education*), which stated:

> For her part Holy Mother Church, in order to fulfill the mandate she received from her divine founder to announce the mystery of salvation to all men and to renew all things in Christ, is under an obligation to promote the welfare of the whole life of man, including his life in this world insofar as it is related to his heavenly vocation, she has therefore a part to play in the development and extension of education.[32]

While the place of the Church and the home in education was considered in this declaration, most of the focus was on the schools, the argument being that due weight should be given "to advances in psychological, pedagogical and intellectual sciences" so that children and young people could "be helped to develop harmoniously their physical, moral and intellectual qualities".[33] This position reflected both the re-evaluation of religious education occurring within the Church internationally and comparable movements in the government and other non-Catholic sectors in relation to the teaching of the 'secular' curriculum subjects.

The early 1960s was a period of change and challenge for most teachers. It was recognized that religious education in Catholic schools could not be the only subject failing to respond to new understandings and insights that reduced or eliminated memory work and encouraged investigation and discussion. Throughout Australia, teachers of religion in Catholic schools began meeting on a regular basis to share ideas and discuss mutual problems. These developments, which took place in the years following the period considered in this book, led to the emergence of another stage yet again in the history of the teaching of religion in Catholic schools in Australia; a stage which Flynn has identified as that of 'experiential catechesis, otherwise known as the stage of the 'life-centered' or 'anthropological' approach.[34]

The Infusion of 'Secular' Subjects with Religious Content

The official position of the Catholic Church was that a major emphasis should be placed not only on religious instruction, but also on ensuring that the climate of schools would be one in which religion would be all-pervasive. This atmosphere was to be maintained in a number of ways, one of which was through the promotion of Catholic viewpoints when teaching the various subjects on the curriculum. Mother Evangelista of the Ursuline Sisters in Sydney gave voice to this stance when, in 1936, she stated:

> Christian education implies the whole field of instruction to be energised and vitalised by religion, and all brands of knowledge must expand in closest relation with divine truth. It embraces and includes every manifestation of God, whether in nature, in history or in life.[35]

The same theme was taken up the following year in a national syllabus of religious instruction, as follows:

Under the system of education in Australia, where the programme, at least in our secondary departments, is not wholly of our own choice, additional caution must be observed. Religion and the profane branches must be intimately associated, running together in the organic growth of the child's knowledge...Our whole culture, European civilization itself, is a gift of Our Holy Mother the Church. Literature, science, history, every subject of our curriculum, may be Christianised.[36]

This echoed the position regularly emanating from the Vatican. Pius IX spoke of the necessity of having all branches of learning "expand in closest alliance with religion",[37] Leo XIII of "every discipline being thoroughly permeated and ruled by religion",[38] and Pius XI of "all the teaching , the whole organization of the school...its teachers, syllabus and text books in every branch";[39] being regulated by the Christian spirit. Thus, it is not surprising that many of those who attended Catholic schools during the period under consideration have recalled that they seemed to be constantly doing projects with an element of God or a picture of God in them.

In an effort to give effect to the official Church position, the *Syllabus of Religious Instruction in Schools*, published in 1950 for all Catholic schools in Victoria, stressed the importance of religious instruction being correlated with other subject areas. The Introduction directed that "pupils' studies should be Christocentric", arguing that:

The schools will endeavour to correlate Christian Doctrine with other subjects, particularly Literature, Social Studies, Science and Nature Study in order that every subject be permeated with Christian piety.[40]

Suggestions were also made as to how this correlation could take place. The following was suggested for grade eight level:

English
    Children's World, Part III
    Lecturettes and compositions on Religious Topics
    Verse Speaking
    Anthologies of Poetry
    Reading the Gospel

Geography
    The Holy Land
    The Missions and Catholic Shrines

Hygiene
>   Religious Motives for the Care of Health

Science
>   Things in Me That Make Me a Believer

Civics
>   Religious Motives for Good Citizenship
>   Introduction to Social Principles

Latin
>   The Mass[41]

Similar suggestions were repeated for all secondary school classes.

History was considered to be a subject of central importance in trying to correlate religious instruction with what were termed the 'secular subjects' on the curriculum. Taking up this point, Massam points out that the Church promoted the teaching of history, because its authority rested on the interpretation of tradition as much as on scripture.[42] Thus, Australian Catholic schools paid great attention to highlighting a Catholic perspective when teaching officially prescribed state history curricula. In dealing with Florence Nightingale, for example, teachers were urged to mention the Catholic religious orders which sent nurses to the Crimea, while they were also warned against using books which "reek with the Protestant tradition" and those written by "bigoted historians".[43]

In 1934 the Catholic Education Office in Melbourne gained government approval for its own history syllabus as a result of its criticisms of the government syllabus This ensued in history being outlined as a component of the *Syllabus of Religious Instruction*. New Catholic History Readers were also produced for use in the schools.[44] The clear message in these readers was that throughout the ages Catholicism was a repository of truth and wisdom. Each reader's cover showed a dove, a cross and the papal arms with the inscription, 'Behold I am with You All Days. The Gates of Hell Shall Not Prevail'.[45] The textual focus was on the background out of which Christianity grew. Consequently, much more emphasis was placed on the Bible, on Roman history and on Irish history than was the case in the government history syllabus. Equally, as Musgrave argues, there was far less emphasis on "the growth of Britain, particularly in its social and economic aspects, and on its expansion to the White Dominions—England overseas; instead, the 'Readers' "focussed on the spread of Christianity and the development of the Catholic Church in Europe and thence its spread to Australia".[46]

In dealing with the spread of Christianity to Australia the emphasis in the readers was on glorifying the work of the Catholic Church in building the country. Pioneer priests and bishops were suggested as worthy of recognition alongside Australia's explorers. For example, one of the *Readers* contained a short chapter entitled 'The Friends of the Convicts', which dealt with Fathers Therry and Ullathorn, the first priests in New South Wales; another had a chapter entitled 'Australia's First Bishop', which was about the Englishman Bishop Polding; while another had a section on 'Missions in New Guinea', with a photograph of the first Papuan priests, and a chapter on 'The Church in Victoria (1901–47)'. The focus, unlike in government schools, was not so much on the export of British democracy to Australia as on the way in which Australians had struggled to build their own democratic system.

Catholic teachers around the country constantly received suggestions as to how religious content in a wide variety of subjects could be built around textbooks not specifically prepared for use in Catholic schools. In articles in *Our Studies*, the journal produced for teachers in Christian Brothers' schools, brothers were urged to raise awareness of Mary, the Blessed Virgin, in English literature, while other publications stressed the importance of reminding students that authors such as G. K. Chesterton were proud of being Catholic. The teaching of geography, as Massam reminds us, could be adjusted with unashamed ease through various remarks aimed at giving it a distinctive religious bias. Also, a certain amount of material with religious content aimed at supplementing 'secular' textbooks was regularly produced for pupils. The following extract from a 1940 issue of *The Children's World*, a school newspaper produced for pupils in Victoria eight times a year by the Catholic Education Office in Melbourne, is illustrative of the approach taken in such works to ensure that matters of religion permeated learning in the variety of subjects on the curriculum:

If you go into the country during the holidays be very careful of snakes as
they have been very busy already this year. Do not forget to say a 'Prayer to
your Guardian Angel' every day and he will protect you. [47]

The overall thrust of the articles in this school newspaper "counselled
pious practices, particularly devotion to Our Lady, detailed the heroic
deeds of missionaries and saints, and serialised those of Wopsy, the
guardian angel".[48]

Overall, then, the Catholic Church in Australia emphasized the
importance of promoting and reinforcing Church doctrine and belief
when teaching any school subject. In 1949 the nation's bishops gave
explicit expression to this position when they reported to Rome that
in Catholic schools religion "permeates all subjects of the curriculum".
Yet it is important not to assume that this was always put into
practice. As Praetz puts it, "the bishops' statement reflected a vision
rather than a reality".[49] She goes on to argue that the bishops were
concerned that much work which could have been undertaken along
the lines they favored was not taking place because of the "use of
secularist textbooks for examinations; excessive eagerness to obtain
results in examinations; excessive advertisement of examination
results and undue competition between Catholic schools, obscuring the
Catholic view of education". This, of course, was because examination
success provided a route to upward social mobility for Catholics,
particularly through joining the public service. The contradiction for
the bishops was that while one of the major reasons for establishing
Catholic schools in Australia in the first instance had been to combat
the development of a materialistic orientation to life amongst 'the
faithful', they also sought social mobility for their flock.

The All-pervasive Religious Atmosphere of the Schools

While the infusion of the 'secular subjects' with Catholic content was
important in maintaining a religious atmosphere in the schools, the
Church also utilized a variety of other practices to this end. A number
of these involved constant surveillance of pupils. Such surveillance
was considered necessary because of the stress within Catholicism on

following the Church's rules and regulations as a means to salvation. The associated practices operated at two levels. The 'upper level' involved 'religious inspectors' regularly visiting schools. These inspectors were priests specially appointed by the bishops to visit all Catholic schools, both primary and secondary, in their respective dioceses to ensure that appropriate programs of religious instruction were being followed. Much more powerful, however, was the constant supervision carried out by the classroom teachers to ensure that their pupils did not stray from the 'straight and narrow'.

The ideology which underpinned the emphasis placed on teachers keeping their pupils constantly under surveillance was the doctrine of original sin. This doctrine contended that children were naturally inclined towards evil. To this was added the contemporary Catholic view in Australia of "society at large as secular, hostile, or indifferent to the truths of religion guarded by the Catholic Church".[50] Yet the position was not totally negative. For one thing, there was the belief that as long as the Church controlled its own schools, there would be a greater chance of its truths being passed on to succeeding generations. On its own, however, this was not considered to be a sufficient safeguard. Thus, great stress was placed on the notion that proper adult surveillance was also necessary to ensure that the child was steered along the path of goodness and righteousness.

There were at least three major approaches taken in providing this surveillance. The first approach calls to mind King and Brownell's argument that, around the world, church-sponsored schools have tended to eliminate content which mentions the particular religion or church unfavorably; which treats a particular topic or subject in what in the church's view, is an immoral manner; or which portrays a way of life that is repugnant to the church.[51] There are records of the various ways in which this operated in the Archdiocese of Melbourne. They include the director of the Catholic Education office of Victoria making representation to relevant government officials about what was seen as anti-Catholic and immoral content prescribed as examination topics, and the issue by the Office of 'supplementary commentaries' to schools to ensure that the Catholic viewpoint was offered to counteract the religious or moral position taken in certain prescribed textbooks.[52] The nuns, religious brothers and priests who taught in the schools were regularly reminded to ensure vigilant supervision over the books which were brought into the schools, "lest through indiscriminate reading danger can be occasioned to faith or morals".[53]

The second major way in which adult guidance was provided for pupils to steer them away from sin was by ensuring they were constantly occupied. On this, the 'Rule' of the Sisters of Saint Joseph of the Most Sacred Heart of Jesus stated:

> The Sisters must be very conscientious in the supervision of the playground, which must never be left without a Sister. Much harm may be done by a few minutes' neglect of this important duty. It would be sad to think that through our negligence an innocent soul was tarnished, and maybe lost.[54]

The Rules of the Christian Brothers took up the same theme, stating that "the pupils should be constantly employed; as soon as one exercise is finished, they should begin the next without any unnecessary delay".[55] Similarly, it was stated that "outside the classroom, too, in the playground and such places, each Brother shall carefully watch over the pupils, so as to shield them from moral and physical danger".

The nature of Australian Catholicism at the time was such that references of this nature to 'moral danger' were equated largely with 'dangers to sexual morality'. This position was reinforced by the official Church insistence on segregated education for the sexes, wherever possible, from the senior levels of primary education onwards. Such segregation, while deemed necessary in order to protect the children from what were seen as their own evil sexual impulses, was also necessary to minimize contact between male and female teachers who were members of religious orders so that their vows of chastity would not be threatened.

The segregation of the sexes in Catholic schools had its origins in the early part of the nineteenth century, when the religious orders first became involved in education in Australia. Most of the orders defined their work as being concerned with the education of boys only or girls only. Some concessions were made, most notably in rural areas where low enrolments would have made single-sex schooling nonviable. Overall, however, Church policy was galvanized with the publication of Pope Pius XI's encyclical *The Christian Education of Youth*, in 1929. In focusing on what it called "modern aberrations", the encyclical criticized "co-education" as "a promiscuous herding together of males and females on a completely equal footing".[56] This was a reiteration of the familiar argument of the Church that bringing the sexes together in their 'formative years' would provide them with both temptations and opportunities to commit 'sins of the flesh'. Thus, it is not surprising to note that the director of Catholic Education in Victoria emphasized the importance of teachers to ensure that "negative influences" were excluded from the schools by "watching the school playground and preventing groups forming, and ruling against 'cliques' that seek privacy away from other children".[57] In a similar vein, it was emphasized that steps should be taken to ensure speedy use of the lavatories and the keeping of hands above the desk.

The third way in which pupils came under surveillance was through practices which brought them to regulate their own behavior through guilt. Statues of religious figures stood guard over them at various vantage points around the school, while scattered along classroom walls and corridors were images of Jesus and the Blessed Virgin, whose faces were depicted in such a manner that their gaze seemed to be constantly on pupils even when the teacher's attention was elsewhere. Cards carrying the same images in miniature form were used as prizes and encouragement awards in Catholic schools, and were kept by pupils in their prayer books, or were displayed in their bedrooms. All of this served to reinforce in pupils' minds that their misdeeds would not go unnoticed in the divine log which was being constantly updated and which would be wheeled out when they had to account for their actions on the 'final day of judgment'. Similarly, while it was constantly impressed on pupils that each one of them had a 'guardian angel' whose job it was to watch over them physically, morally and spiritually, they were reminded also that this perfect being could report their misdemeanors to heaven for recording.

So far, this account has centered on the surveillance practices which operated to ensure that schools had a religious atmosphere which was all-encompassing. Other practices, however, also operated to this end. In particular, there were practices aimed at regularly intensifying the religious commitment of pupils. Some of these corresponded to what McLaren has termed "rituals of revitalization" and "rituals of intensification".[58] Rituals of revitalization were intended to renew motivation and values through, for example, the annual school religious retreat. This event, generally lasting about three days, involved students immersing themselves in prayer, religious reflection, spiritual exercises and the reading of religious works. Students' religious zeal was also revitalized at this time through studying the lives of founders of religious orders and the history of the orders themselves.

Revitalization also took place through the preparation for, and participation in, Gregorian chant competitions between schools. Other drama-laden practices included attending special 'High Masses' at various stages in the school year either in the school itself or in the nearby parish church, preparing for the services of Holy Week and Easter, holding elaborate processions on the feast days of various saints, and preparing pupils for the sacraments of Confirmation and Holy Communion. The sacrament of Confession came in for special emphasis; pupils were encouraged in the schools to confess regularly and they were trained in the preparation ritual. This involved a systematic examination of conscience, in which they reviewed their behavior with regard to God, other individuals and themselves. Because of the practice of frequent attendance at Confession, and through the encouragement of regular self-denial, pupils were constantly reminded that a fresh beginning was always possible as long as they were truly sorry for their sins and sincere in their desire to mend their ways.

'Rituals of intensification' were also practiced. These were aimed at recharging teachers and students emotionally. Each class began with a prayer, followed by appropriate aspirations, while classes stopped on the ringing of a mid-day bell to recite the long Prayer of the Angelus. Also, the constitutions of particular religious teaching orders laid down strict rules as to the manner in which the day should be organized around prayer. The Presentation Sisters were required to engage in spiritual recollection at noon each day. Similarly, the Christian Brothers were required upon entering the classroom each morning to kneel and recite privately the 'Prayer Before School', while they stopped classes every hour to recite The Hail Mary with the pupils.

Other practices also operated to intensify the religious atmosphere of schools. Teachers regularly eulogized the life of nuns, brothers or priests, portraying it as bordering on being saintly because of their commitment to the consecrated celibate state. Pupils' religious zeal was intensified through the pride instilled from belonging to the various pious associations organized in the schools. These included the Apostleship of Prayer, the Sacred Heart Association, the Confraternity of the Divine Child, and the Missionary Association of the Holy Childhood. A more select group was invited to join sodalities like the Children of Mary. These were special prayer and devotional groups. Fogarty has described them as follows:

> The sodalities, in the hands of the Church, were special training grounds within the general training of the school; they aimed at cultivating higher ideals and stressed the obligation of self-improvement and of using one's influence for good, thereby turning to account the latent capacities of leadership, stimulating them and directing them to the common good. Essentially the sodalities were for a small nucleus, an elite; they were to act as cells exercising an influence for good upon the larger organism.[59]

School journals regularly published photographs of enrolled pupils, accompanied by laudatory accounts of their activities. The most select group of all was invited to join organizations like the Legion of Mary. Arnold has recalled her membership as follows:

> The Legion was conducted along the lines of a Roman legion, with brass banners of the imperial eagle standing puissant over the sign, *Legio Marie*...Members of the Legion were bound to convert non-believers to Christianity. They were expected to descend, always in pairs, into dens of anti-Catholicism to try to convince unbelievers of the truth of the Church.[60]

Members of the Legion of Mary were required to be very secretive about their activities. While they kept minutes of their meetings, these were not freely available. Members were also instructed on the need to preserve absolute secrecy in regard to any issues debated at meetings.

Some students were involved in the Catholic Action movement through their membership of school branches of the Young Catholic Students' (YCS) society, established in many primary and secondary schools in 1942. The aim of this society was "to change and Christianize the environment of school boys and school girls" through "Gospel discussion, 'contact and influence', leaders, sub-leaders, teams, activity groups and general meetings".[61] This activity was coordinated and organized by a permanent national secretary attached to the National Catholic Secretariat in Melbourne. It complemented a whole range of other extra-curricular activities, including the operation of Catholic sports' leagues and a Catholic press.

Rituals of intensification also focused on missionary work. Pupils were organized to raise money through concerts and bazaars, while school magazines appealed to their idealism with photographs of missionaries in Africa, Asia and Latin America, and with accounts of their heroic activities in foreign lands. Through such practices, Catholic schools also differed from government schools by promoting the asexual consecrated virginal state for those who were members of religious orders as the highest state one could achieve in this life. This will be discussed in detail in the following chapter.

Notes

[1]   Sisters of Saint Joseph of the Most Sacred Heart of Jesus, *Customs and Practices of the Sisters of St. Joseph of the Most Sacred Heart of Jesus*, p. 14.

[2]   R. Fogarty, *Catholic Education in Australia: 1806–1950* (Melbourne: Melbourne University Press, 1959), p. 389.

[3]   The Brigidine Sisters, *Directory of the Brigidine Sisters* (New South Wales, Australia: The Brigidine Sisters, 1955), p. 47.

[4]   Sisters of Saint Joseph of the Most Sacred Heart of Jesus, *Customs and Practices of the Sisters of St. Joseph of the Most Sacred Heart of Jesus*, p. 7.

[5]   See M. Flynn, *The Culture of Catholic Schools* (Homebush, NSW, Australia: St. Paul's Publications, 1993).

[6]   K. Lawlor, 'Bishop Bernard D. Stewart and resistance to the reform of religious education in the Diocese of Sandhurst, 1950–1979' (unpublished Ph.D. thesis, La Trobe University, 1999), p. 258.

[7]   Ibid.

[8]   E. Campion, 'Irish religion in Australia', *The Australasian Catholic Record*, Vol. 55, No. 1, 1978, p. 11.

[9]   Ibid.

10 H. Praetz, *Building a School System: A Sociological Study of Catholic Education* (Melbourne: Melbourne University Press, 1980), p. 33.

11 Ibid.

12 Ibid.

13 This definition of 'apologetics' is given in A. S. Bryk, V. E. Lee and P. B. Holland, *Catholic Schools and the Common Good* (Cambridge: Harvard University Press, 1993), p. 4.

14 Ibid.

15 J. Whyte, *Church and State in Modern Ireland* (Dublin: Gill and Macmillan, 1971), p. 16.

16 Ibid.

17 Ibid.

18 Ibid.

19 K. Lawlor, 'Bishop Bernard D. Stewart and resistance to the reform of religious education in the Diocese of Sandhurst, 1950–1979', p. 261.

20 Ibid.

21 This is dealt with in R. Fogarty, *Catholic Education in Australia: 1806–1950*, pp. 383–402.

22 Ibid.

23 See, for example, J. T. McMahon, 'A liturgical programme for schools', *Australasian Catholic Record*, Vol. 8, No. 4, 1931, pp. 297–304.

24 See 'Address to Annual Teachers' Conference, Perth, 1940' in box marked 'Rev. J. T. McMahon', Archdiocese of Perth Archives. Perth, Australia.

25 See J. Bruner, *The Process of Education* (New York: Vantage, 1960).

26 See 'Address to Annual Teachers' Conference, Perth, 1940'.

27 A. Tormey, *Teaching Orders in Catholic Education in Western Australia 1955–1975: A Historical Study of Changes and Repercussions* (unpublished M.Ed. thesis, The University of Western Australia, 1976), pp. 27–28.

28 R. Fogarty, *Catholic Education in Australia: 1806–1950*, p. 454.

29 K. Lawlor, 'Bishop Bernard D. Stewart and resistance to the reform of religious education in the Diocese of Sandhurst, 1950–1979', p. 263.

30 Ibid., pp. 263–266.

31 Ibid.

32 See A. Flannery (ed.), *Vatican Council 11. The Conciliar and Post Conciliar Documents* (Dublin: Dominican Publications, 1975), p. 725.

33 Ibid., p. 726.

34 M. Flynn, *The Culture of Catholic Schools*.

35 Quoted in K. Massam, *Sacred Threads: Catholic Spirituality in Australia 1922–1962* (Sydney: University of New South Wales Press, 1996), p. 41.

36 M. B. Hanrahan, 'A definite syllabus of religious instruction with regional variations', Australian Catholic Education Congress, *Australian Catholic Education Congress, Adelaide, Australia* (Melbourne: The Advocate Press, 1937), p. 102.

37 Quoted in R. Fogarty, *Catholic Education in Australia: 1806–1950*, p. 410.

38 Ibid.

39 Ibid.

[40] H. Praetz, *Building a School System: A Sociological Study of Catholic Education*, p. 26.

[41] Ibid

[42] K. Massam, *Sacred Threads: Catholic Spirituality in Australia 1922–1962*, p. 42.

[43] Ibid.

[44] Victorian Catholic Education Office, *Catholic History Readers* (6 vols.). (Melbourne: Advocate Press, n.d.).

[45] Ibid.

[46] P. W. Musgrave, 'To be an Australian? Secular and Catholic versions of national identity in primary school textbooks, 1895–1964' (unpublished paper, School of Graduate Studies, Monash University, 1993), p. 30.

[47] This newspaper was founded in 1936.

[48] H. Praetz, *Building a School System: A Sociological Study of Catholic Education*, p. 28.

[49] Ibid., p. 25.

[50] Ibid., p. 143.

[51] A. R. King and J. A. Brownell. *The Curriculum and the Disciplines of Knowledge* (New York: John Wiley and Sons, 1966).

[52] H. Praetz, *Building a School System: A Sociological Study of Catholic Education*, p. 16.

[53] The Brigidine Sisters, *Directory of the Brigidine Sisters* (New South Wales: The Brigidine Sisters, 1955), p. 55.

[54] Sisters of Saint Joseph of the Most Sacred Heart of Jesus, *Customs and Practices of the Sisters of St. Joseph of the Most Sacred Heart of Jesus*, p. 8.

[55] *Directory and Rules of the Congregation of the Brothers of the Christian Schools of Ireland* (Dublin: The Christian Brothers, 1927), p. 258.

[56] Pope Pius XI, *The Christian Education of Youth* (London: Catholic Truth Society, 1970).

[57] H. Praetz, *Building a School System: A Sociological Study of Catholic Education*, p. 28.

[58] P. McLaren, 'Making Catholics: The ritual production of conformity in a Catholic junior high school', *Journal of Education*, Vol. 168, No. 2, 1986, p. 66.

[59] R. Fogarty, *Catholic Education in Australia 1806–1950*, p. 413.

[60] J. Arnold, *Mother Superior Woman Inferior* (Blackburn, Victoria, Australia: Dove Communications, 1985), p. 141.

[61] R. Fogarty, *Catholic Education in Australia 1806–1950*, p. 415.

Chapter Five

The Construction of Gender in Australian Catholic Schools

The central argument of this chapter is that the construction of gender in Catholic schools in Australia during the period 1922–65 has to be viewed primarily as having been influenced by religious considerations. In this area, the process of education differed sharply from that in government schools and schools run by other religious denominations. As the first section of this chapter demonstrates, pupils were regularly reminded that within the Church's hierarchy of vocations, to be a nun, religious brother or priest, was to occupy a role higher than that of the lay person. The chapter then goes on to argue that while the personal qualities emphasized for the lay Catholic population matched Australian stereotypes in a variety of ways, what gave them their distinctive mark was that they were justified with religious arguments.

The Promotion of the Consecrated Celibate Life

The construction of gender in Catholic schools in Australia differed significantly from that in state schools and schools run by other religious denominations insofar as pupils were regularly reminded that the Church valued nuns, brothers and priests more than it did lay people. Teachers who were members of religious orders played a major role in this process. They subtly introduced students to the religious way of life through the manner in which they led them to follow some of its rhythms, with the school year being largely organized around the religious calendar and significant events being timetabled to coincide with the feast days of saints.

Teachers were required by their religious superiors to create opportunities whereby pupils could be encouraged to "enter religious life", as it was put. On this, the *Directory of the Brigidine Sisters* instructed as follows:

> School Sodalities, zealously worked, serve to create the atmosphere in which religious vocations are most securely developed. Nowhere is it reasonable to expect so many Postulants for our Congregation as in our own schools. If it be right and prudent to enquire from girls what particular secular pursuit they desire to follow, it is certainly proper to ask that child, whom grace seems to mark out among her companions, if she feels disposed towards the Religious Life.[1]

The Sisters of Saint Joseph of the Most Sacred Heart of Jesus were even more directive, insisting that one day in each month special prayers were to be said in their schools for divine intercession "to ensure a supply of good vocations".[2] The Christian Brothers were urged to "seek to lead generous and pious youths to devote their lives to God's service as priests in the work of the Ministry, or as religious in the cause of Catholic education".[3] Brothers in charge of senior classes were given even more explicit instructions, being told that they should avail themselves of school libraries, short annual retreats, school sodalities, "zealous instruction on the advantages of the religious state" and the maintenance of a religious atmosphere in the schools, in order to "foster vocations to the priesthood and to the religious life".[4]

It was quite common for teachers who were members of religious orders to speak to pupils in class about the lives of fellow religious as a heroic sacrifice. Their work was portrayed as being extraordinarily difficult, yet borne with a cheerful spirit because it brought them closer than lay people to God. Passages in the 'rules' and 'constitutions' of religious orders could be called upon for neat summaries expressing the ends of what was referred to as the "noble calling" of those in religious life. The Brigidine Sisters learned that their order had the following aim:

> The greater glory of God, that the members of it may not only apply themselves to attain their own salvation, but also employ themselves with all their power in promoting the spiritual improvement of their neighbour, by affording Religious and Secular education to children, and all such persons as may present themselves for instruction, in the truths of our Holy Religion.[5]

Similarly, the position of the Sisters of Mercy was that the "special object of the Congregation is the salvation of souls" and "the spirit of the Congregation is mercy towards those who are afflicted with ignorance, suffering, and other like miseries".[6]

The glorification of the lives of nuns, brothers and priests through the schools was no more than a reflection of the practice adopted by the Church with the adult 'faithful'. As Kennedy reminds us, Archbishop Duhig of Brisbane was only echoing a common refrain in 1933 when he told a gathering of lay Catholic women that any role they might take up could only be secondary to that of women religious: "We must never forget that in the forefront of women's work in Australia there are 10,000 consecrated Virgins of Christ".[7] The Catholic newspapers, in heroic terms, regularly reported groups of young nuns, brothers and priests heading off for mission stations in New Guinea, the Solomon Islands and India, amongst other places. In a similar vein, the literature which priests made available on marriage to engaged couples stressed that the consecrated virginity of the religious life was a privileged gift, while the great majority would have to settle for the good but 'ordinary' state of marriage. Such an attitude was also regularly expressed publicly in terms which echoed those of Cardinal Gilroy, when, in 1963, he encouraged parents "to pray that God would give to their daughters the inestimable privilege of a call to religious life".[8]

In promoting the consecrated religious state as the most noble and holy state one could achieve in this life, the Catholic Church, as Massam[9] argues, was simply following a general bureaucratic trend in its preference for non-salaried celibate workers who had no responsibilities other than their jobs. The Church made no attempt to deny this position; indeed, those who had the role of visiting schools to encourage students to consider joining their respective religious orders stressed that the celibate state was the superior one as it freed nuns, brothers and priests from family responsibilities so that they could devote themselves totally to God's work on earth. The special 'recruiting agents' were themselves either nuns, brothers or priests, and had spent a considerable amount of time "in the service of the Church", as they were wont to put it. Quite often they had also spent time "on the missions" and appealed to the youthful sentiments of their audiences with tales of their deeds in exotic places, accompanied by maps, photographs and slide shows aimed at exciting the adventurous minds of adolescents.

The religious orders distributed recruitment literature amongst pupils through the schools, the parishes and the Catholic press. This literature appealed to a wide range of sentiment. A booklet produced by the Sisters of Saint Joseph of the Most Sacred Heart of Jesus[10] in 1948, for example, started out by appealing to the caring side of young women, informing them that the order was engaged in teaching 38,373 children in schools, in looking after 1,264 boys and girls "who have no parents to care for them", and in ensuring that 165 destitute adults were being "sheltered and protected". To this were added appeals to heroism by calling others to join the existing 1,746 Sisters in their "wonderful work", appeals to sacrifice by stating that "if there was just one more Sister, the teachings of the Church could be brought to more souls", and appeals to guilt by the use of such rhetorical questions as "Are you ready to help?"[11] The all-important nature of the enterprise was justified in simple yet fundamental terms: "Souls are the most precious things in the world. Our Divine Savior suffered and died for souls. A girl who becomes a Sister of Saint Joseph helps to save many souls".

The notion of "self-offering"[12] was also promoted in the recruitment literature. A booklet produced by the 'Congregations of Religious Women in Western Australia' gave expression to this position in the following rather dramatic tone: "Cut through me, Lord, strip me of all this selfish self, fire me a little with your generous love—in fact, take me over, and use me as you will".[13] What was being eulogized was what was termed the "total commitment" made by those who joined a religious order; a commitment to love and to being of service to those in need.

Various literary devices were used in the recruitment literature to impress upon readers the enormity of the commitment they were being called upon to make. Some of it lent itself itself to constant repetition and thus entering the subconscious. A booklet distributed by the Sisters of Mercy stated that a member of the order could be described as "one who serves, one who loves, one who carries the light" in schools, hospitals, hostels and orphanages, and in clerical, domestic and social work. It then asked why one would want to follow this path and answered as follows in chant-like fashion:

—To show Christ to the world wherever I go
—To be all things to those in need, the little ones, the homeless, the
   suffering, ignorant, poor and distressed
—To point the way to God for many many souls
—To give all for love in joyful service. [14]

It was also common to hold up the founder or foundress of the order as an exemplar of heroism, as someone who had turned his or her back on the pleasures of the world in order to serve God and serve those in need.

Care was taken by recruiters and by those who produced the recruitment literature to balance the 'self-offering' appeal of the religious life with more 'human' attractions, lest they be seen as advocating a commitment to a life of misery. Foremost in these attractions was the community life of the religious. The various booklets disseminated contained photographs of happy smiling groups at recreation, or sitting together at prayer.[15] These photographs regularly contained a mix of ages, with elderly members creating an image of the cloister as a place of security and homeliness for their younger peers. Such visual representations were accompanied by texts which spoke of community life being attractive because everybody shared the same ideals. Nor was it a life portrayed as being without drama, a situation represented most vividly in recruitment talks and accompanying literature on females becoming 'brides of Christ':

> A religious life is far more wonderful than any career in the world. To be a Sister of St. Joseph, the Bride of Jesus! To live in close intimacy with the Son of God! To labour for Him! To belong only to Him! To win souls for heaven! Could anything be more glorious?[16]

Poetry, as in the following example, was also used to generate a notion that in becoming a 'bride of Christ' one would be led to a state of serenity and tranquility:

> She swings the incense in her thought
> Before the quiet throne of God;
> He is the lover she has sought
> She finds Him where no foot has trod
> She hears him where no voice is heard
> For she has gone the secret way
> Only the innocent may go,
> And she has learned the secret word
> Only the innocent may say;
> Time passes gently by her—so
> Her days are like the quiet tune
> Of waters that go murmuring by,
> When in the fragrant lap of June
> The indolent green meadows lie.[17]

This image of living a calm regulated life was balanced by one of excitement on the mission fields. Such excitement was held out as being within reach of those attracted to working in exotic locations through accounts in mission magazines of churches, hospitals and schools being built deep in the jungle or on the shores of palm-fringed tropical beaches.

The recruitment literature also hinted at a certain theological justification for the Church's valuing of the way of life of nuns, brothers and priests more than that of lay people. These hints were along the lines of the following extract from a recruitment pamphlet produced by the Sisters of Saint Joseph of the Most Sacred Heart of Jesus and distributed nationally throughout their schools:

If you have a vocation, our Lord is offering you a life of happiness greater than you ever dreamed of, happiness that will never fail. The pleasure the world promises you will never content your heart.[18]

Occasionally the hints were offered in a more attractive poetic form:

Forget your ease and comfort
Come and follow me
Down the paths that I have trod
A new life you will see.[19]

Such a form of presentation heightened the attraction of the unique quality of religious life which would be revealed on joining the order. Yet, the precise nature of this quality could not be made too explicit at this stage lest it act as a deterrent to those who might be contemplating joining.

Once aspirants joined a religious order the notion of what made religious life an elevated one began to reveal itself through the great stress placed on renouncing one's sexual role and function to attain a neutral personhood. The rule of the Loreto order summarized this view as follows:

Let them always remember to how sublime a state they are called by Almighty God; and, for that reason, their main design must be, by a perfect beauty and purity of soul, to please Him more and more, and by avoiding, with the greatest care, all willful sins, to render themselves acceptable in his eyes…Concupiscence being the root of all evils, they are seriously to extirpate and root it entirely out of their hearts; and to this effect they must divest themselves of all carnal love and affection for parents and relations, and for other creatures, and only have that love for them which a well-ordered charity requires of them—as persons that are dead to the world and self-love, and that live only to Christ our Lord, whom they have instead of parents, brethern, and all things else.[20]

Religious orders promoted achievement of such an asexual personhood as intimately connected with achieving the holiness which allowed one to transcend nature and partake in the eschatological realm. In the case of nuns, it also allowed them to occupy certain traditional male roles. At the most obvious level, they became school principals at a time when this position was largely seen in the non-Catholic sector as being the preserve of men, except in the case of all-girls' schools. At a less obvious level, it was not unusual for nuns in full religious garb to train boys' 'footy' teams in country areas where they had coeducational classes in small secondary schools or secondary-tops attached to primary schools. By contrast, it was considered most inappropriate for female teachers in state schools, other than specialist physical education teachers, to have any involvement in such a male dominated sport.

From considerations so far, it is clear that within the Church's hierarchy of vocations, a nun, brother or priest was considered higher than a lay person. It is also clear that, publicly, great emphasis was placed on this position. What did not receive public expression, however, was that further hierarchies existed within the ranks of those in religious life itself. The hierarchy based on the patriarchal nature of religious life stands out in this regard, as those who were ordained priests occupied a much more elevated place than did brothers and nuns. This led to great tension within the Catholic Church in Australia in the nineteenth century, due in particular to the almost total obedience which priests and bishops demanded of nuns and brothers. The extent of the unequal power relations which existed and the consequences these had for the nuns has been aptly summarized by West:

> It was in the Roman Catholic Church that the greatest oppression of women in ministry was experienced at the hands of a male hierarchy. Incident after incident occurred, especially in the Sisters of Charity and the Josephite orders, in which nuns were bullied, intimidated, exploited and even excommunicated by clergy and bishops who were often less godly than they...The basis of this behaviour was the patriarchal system prevailing in the church, which in turn was derived from the sexist ideology of the day which categorised women according to certain suppositions about ability, birth and role...As the Catholic Church and the colonies became more established, 'Leave it to the good sisters' became the familiar cry of the male clergy when sundry tasks arose.[21]

This situation continued to prevail well into the twentieth century and led to the emergence of a great deal of folklore within convents which condemned the priests and bishops concerned and glorified those Reverend Mothers who mounted resistance.

Similar stories were told in the houses of brothers and priests who were members of religious orders, both having received similar, though not quite as extreme, treatment at the hands of diocesan priests and bishops. However, very little if any of the accounts of controversies which ensued got aired in the public domain.[22] In particular, they were rarely spoken about in the schools lest they would act to deter any student from joining a religious order. Rather, there was a constant favorable portrayal of the consecrated celibate life of both males and females.

The Construction of the Unconsecrated Female

While Catholic schools expended great effort on encouraging girls to give serious consideration to becoming nuns, it was recognized that the majority would not choose such a life. Thus, the schools also promoted a model of femininity valorizing the good wife and mother who stayed at home to care for the family. A leading theologian of the day made the Church's role in this regard clear:

> While studying the same subjects as man, she must study them in a different way and for another purpose. For her the study of letters and sciences must be more directly cultural; it should lack the competitive note. It is moreover desirable that in the curriculum of girls' courses of study there should be a decided bias towards the practical arts and accomplishments called into play in the management of the home.[23]

This perspective was also made explicit in the 'rules' and 'constitutions' of religious orders. The Brigidine Sisters, for example, were urged to inculcate in girls "domestic tastes and habits, that if they enter the state of matrimony, they may be able to regulate a household and prove themselves good wives and mothers".[24] In adopting such a position the Catholic Church in Australia was doing no more than emphasizing gender roles which largely matched Australian stereotypes. As West has put it, one of the most significant doctrines influencing the lives not only of Australian women, but Western women in general, from approximately 1850 to 1950, was the Victorian concept of "separate spheres".[25] According to this notion, the man's sphere was the workplace while the woman's sphere was the home.

West argues that women were encouraged to think of themselves as part of a family relationship only, and to come to accept as 'normal' the conventions and prescriptions associated with this relationship.[26] A range of practices was drawn upon in various societies to reinforce this position as the dominant one governing gender relationships and to teach women that the best course of action was to base their existence on their husbands' careers. Some of the more public practices which operated in Australia have been summarized thus:

> In the 1890s depression, when school budgets were severely strained, it was the female teachers who were the first to be dismissed. This situation was to be repeated in the great depression of the 1930s. Until 1947, women were forced to resign from the permanent teaching staff of schools and colleges when they married. This scenario also obtained in banks and many business houses.[27]

Also, up until 1966, women employed by the federal government had to resign permanent positions upon marriage and it was not until the 1970s that they benefited from equal-pay legislation.

Throughout Australian society "the theme of the family as a refuge from an increasingly harsh and alien world"[28] was widely promoted to justify excluding women from large portions of the workforce and to promulgate the notion that staying at home was a more attractive proposition. This took place through a variety of means, including the messages offered in women's magazines and the teaching of domestic science in the schools. Catholic society and Catholic schools mirrored the general trend. What was distinctive about Catholics, however, was that they used religious arguments to justify the emphasis on the domestication of females. The view was that women, despite being absent from decision-making within the Church, occupied a pivotal role since, as mothers, they had a major responsibility for the spiritual welfare of their families and for ensuring that the souls of their children were not endangered.

The importance within Catholicism of the role of the mother within the family was reinforced in the latter half of the nineteenth century as part of the Church's response to modernism. By this stage the Church was very much under siege. It had lost most of its temporal power as a result of the unification of Italy. To compound matters, it was faced with a growing individualism associated with urban industrialization. Such individualism was seen to have the potential to lead to a loosening of the Church's hold over people's minds. The solution was to slow down and even reverse this process through bolstering the family unit and taking control of it.

In maintaining control of the family, the Church focused on the woman and persuaded her that when she got married she should stay in the home. To this end, it perpetuated a notion that women had a natural vocation as housewives and mothers. The message was consistent; if a mother went out to work, family life would be destroyed. Mirroring the international trend, the Catholic Bishops in Australia proclaimed throughout the first half of the twentieth century the notion that the home is the child's first school and that its mother is its first teacher. This position was restated regularly in the Catholic press, as well as from the pulpit, at various religious gatherings and in the schools. Some ground was conceded with the outbreak of World War Two when women were needed to replace the male workforce which had enlisted. After the war, however, Catholic mothers, like most Australian mothers, returned to the household until the radical changes of the 1960s seriously ruptured their traditional home-making roles.

The most common image presented to girls in Catholic schools to impress upon them their role within the household was that of the submissive, other-worldly, and busy Mary, the Blessed Virgin. Nelson and Nelson recall that "the most powerful model was Mary, the paradoxical Virgin and mother. We sang her praises, celebrated her life with numerous feast days, walked in procession behind her decorated statue".[29] Other models of femininity proffered by the nuns to their students were the long-suffering, often oppressed female saints, like St. Monica, the anguished mother of St. Augustine, and the elderly pregnant

St. Elizabeth.[30] Girls had it impressed on them that they should also be 'God's police' in the home. This meant that they would have to make sure their husbands attended Sunday Mass and other devotions held in the parish church, and also that they did not engage in drinking, gambling and other vices. Even more significant was the stress placed on the importance of making sure their children attended a Catholic school, of overseeing their children's memorization of Christian doctrine, and of helping them in their preparation for receiving the sacraments. Girls were encouraged to pray for divine assistance in fulfilling this role. They were also told that when they became mothers they should bless their homes, dedicate them to the Sacred Heart and pray to the Virgin Mary to safeguard their children against the temptations of life.[31]

The expectation, as Kennedy puts it, was that a married woman would be a "chiseler of character, a fashioner of souls".[32] This position was made explicit by the Pope in *Divini Illius Magistri* in 1929, when he highlighted the important role of the mother in the religious, moral and civil training of her children.[33] Overall, the notion was that by making the mother almost solely responsible for the spiritual welfare of the children, the risk to their immortal souls was minimized. In the coeducational settings of the junior levels of primary school, girls and boys were instructed almost exclusively by nuns, so from an early age came to view such religious instruction as being primarily women's work. The majority of pupils eventually proceeded to the single-sex environment of the upper levels of primary schooling, with a minority of these then going on to secondary schools which were also organized along single-sex lines. These environments were conducive to taking one stage further the process of instilling a clear definition of gender roles when it came to religious instruction within the home. In other words, keeping the sexes apart meant that there was no possibility of debate between them in school on the Church's insistence that the mother had the primary responsibility as the guardian of faith and morals in the home. In this way, there was little room for confusion.

Girls and boys learned in their respective single-sex environments that the ultimate authority on matters of faith and morals rested with the priests and bishops. This was impressed upon them through direct instruction, particularly in religion classes. In the case of boys, the notion that ultimate authority in religious matters resided with priests and brothers was reinforced by the insistence on absolute obedience to teaching brothers and priests, a practice which was accompanied by regular corporal punishment. For girls, the association was reinforced by the reverence demanded of them by the nuns towards a priest whenever he entered the school or its environs.

In focusing on this aspect of the education of women, it is important to keep the wider social context in mind. By the 1930s, Catholics in Australia were no longer characteristically poorer than other denominations, even though they were still under-represented in business and higher education. While there was an acceptance within the Church of the class structure in Australian society, the objective was to use the educational system to try to consolidate the position of those who had reached the higher levels, while continuing to encourage upward mobility amongst those at the lower levels. To this end, different religious orders tended to concentrate on teaching different cohorts of pupils within the social strata. Thus, orders like the Sisters of Mercy, the Sisters of Saint Joseph of the Most Sacred Heart of Jesus and the Christian Brothers largely focused on those at the lower end of the spectrum, trying to give them an education which would improve their lot in society and dispel any notion there might still be a relationship between being Catholic and being poor and uneducated. This was important not only for maintaining the loyalty of Catholics themselves, but also in order to make Catholicism more attractive to possible converts.

In the case of girls at the lower level of society, it was seen as important that they obtain some qualification, such as becoming a secretary, nurse, or primary school teacher, so that they would be perceived as dignified not only during their employment phase before getting married, but also in case they ran into difficulty in their marriages and had to fend for themselves and their children. At the other end of the social spectrum were those who were taught by religious orders like the

Jesuits and the Loreto Sisters. Again, in the case of girls at this level of society, education for domestication was still considered very important. For these, however, there was great emphasis on personal development and cultural pursuits; if young married Catholic ladies were to be active in 'society' and move amongst those with influence, then it was important that they be able to partake in debate on an equal footing and thus act as local ambassadors for their religion.

It was impressed on girls and boys, both in school and before they got married, that if their partner was a non-Catholic they were to "do the utmost to effect the conversion of the non-Catholic party" and that together they would have to enter into a prenuptial agreement that all children of both sexes would be baptized Catholics and would be instructed in the Catholic faith. The nature of this agreement was such that the parish priest would be able to inform the bishop there was "a moral certainty" of it being faithfully observed. At the same time, it was made quite clear that 'mixed marriages' were "merely tolerated". By the 1940s, such marriages could not be celebrated before an altar, but rather in the sacristy of the church or in the presbytery. This entrenched position reflected general trends in what was being enacted within the Catholic Church in England and America at the time.

The Construction of the Unconsecrated Male

Just as with girls, Catholic schools accepted that, despite the effort which they expended on encouraging boys to 'enter religious life', the majority would choose not to do so. Therefore, they also promoted a model of what it meant to be a Catholic male. The personal qualities emphasized for boys matched Australian stereotypes to a great extent. In particular, strict discipline and hardship were promoted because of their perceived ability to produce 'hard men'. Indeed, anecdotal evidence suggests that Catholic schools were more excessive than government schools or schools of other religious denominations in this regard. The schools of the Christian Brothers in particular acquired a reputation for ferocious discipline, especially from the 1920s to the 1950s. This reputation, as Coldrey[34] reminds us, is vividly presented in the images permeating the memoirs of 'Australian old boys'. Barry Oakley, one of the country's most significant dramatists during the period, has written of Brother Conroy who delivered "leather fusilades" with his strap "carried gunmanhandy in the hip pocket of his shabby black habit".[35] In similar vein, Laurie Clancy, "a prominent university academic in Melbourne"[36] has described the strap thus:

> It was a vicious looking thing, about 12 inches long and consisting of six or eight black and brown thin strips of dried leather stitched amateurishly together. It was the stitching that was alleged to make it so painful.[37]

Novelist Desmond O'Grady,[38] a former pupil of a Melbourne Catholic college, and Christopher Koch,[39] a former pupil of St. Virgil's College, Hobart, have also related their experiences in what was clearly a tough regime in the 1950s.[40]

Most Catholic boys' schools, like government schools and those of other religious denominations, promoted the army cadets through which boys were able to demonstrate patriotism and were encouraged to be willing to fight and die for their country if necessary. Most Catholic boys' schools also adopted the English belief in team sports for moral training and proving manhood.[41] The view was that these sports were synonymous with assertiveness, aggression, courage and toughness. Yet there seems to have been somewhat less emphasis on the English public school notion of character building through sport and a greater emphasis on the importance of games for keeping boys out of mischief to reduce the possibility of committing 'sins of the flesh'. The successes of boys' teams on the playing field, as with girls' teams, particularly against non-Catholic schools, was widely publicized as part of the Church's grand plan of using the educational system to elevate the social status of Catholics in Australian society. Reporting success in sporting competitions demonstrated to society at large that not only were Catholics a separate segment of Australian society, but also that they could mix it with the best of the rest.

Catholic boys' schools, like government schools and those of other religious denominations, also implicitly inculcated the hegemony of men over women. They reinforced the view that a married woman's place was in the home. They also promoted the notion that a successful Catholic male was someone who, in public, was accompanied by a wife who was a passive onlooker rather than a participant and an equal. Here it is useful to recall Connell's[42] point that one crucial way that adolescent boys learn masculinity from their peers and mentors is by distancing themselves from women and differentiating themselves as sharply as possible from traits and behaviors deemed effeminate. This process, as Brice[43] reminds us, was observable in all schools during the period in question, but Catholic boys' schools carried it out with exceptional thoroughness:

> Not only were there no women teachers in Catholic boys' secondary schools, the religious orders often included lay brothers, who performed the domestic and other menial functions of a boarding college elsewhere performed by women. Hence they were *totally* male worlds—women were excluded, unquestioningly the *other*.[44]

Thus, Brice concludes, Catholic boys' schools implicitly conveyed the notion that "growing up into manhood entailed distancing oneself from womanhood and femininity, and accepting that men were superior, women subordinate".[45]

The account so far suggests that the practice of keeping the sexes apart in Catholic schools at the senior levels of primary school, as well as in secondary school, can be seen as a practice perpetuating male hegemony over women. It also acted to complement the model of the family put before girls. Boys, like girls, were offered the image of the Holy Family as one upon which they should base their own lives. Yet, they also had to develop an image of the ideal wife before they could be permitted to associate freely with women. A coeducational environment would certainly not have been conducive to this task, since boys might become confused by too much sexual attraction and be tempted just as Adam was tempted by Eve in the Garden of Eden.

The dominant feminine image put before Catholic boys was that of the Virgin Mary, symbol of a traditional concept of appropriate womanhood. She was often venerated, particularly in boys' schools, in courageous terms, "with all the love of an affectionate son, and with all the devoutness of a chivalrous knight".[46] This veneration was reinforced through membership of organizations like the Legion of Mary which, for adolescents, had single-sex membership and met after school. From the very beginning, boys in the Legion of Mary learned that the following was the "spirit of the Legion":

> Especially does the Legion aspire after her [the Blessed Virgin's] profound humility, her perfect obedience, her angelical sweetness, her continual prayer, her universal mortification, her altogether spotless purity, her heroic patience, her heavenly wisdom, her self-sacrificing courageous love of God, and above all her faith, that virtue which has in her alone been found in its utmost extent and never equaled.[47]

Boys also learned to expect wives to be like Mary in terms of these qualities. For boys then, just as for girls, the family was romanticized in various ways. Mothers and Mary were idealized for their 'gentle sway' in matters domestic. Notions of the virtues of purity and modesty were regularly promoted, while the "evils of divorce" were highlighted. All of this served to reinforce the Church's emphasis on the need to bolster the family unit and take control of it, so that, in turn, control was maintained over the minds of the 'faithful'.

Various practices operated to develop Catholic boys' emotional commitment to the family. Thus, as Hamilton puts it, the masculinity which was encouraged differed from the hegemonic Anglo-Saxon one in some important ways:

> It was aggressive and passive, militant and sentimental, public and private...On the football field the students were encouraged to fight for their faith, while as members of sodalities compose sentimental verse.[48]

One objective of the sodalities for boys was to kindle an aspiration to the priesthood and establish habits of Catholic piety and service. At meetings they discussed religious topics and vowed to be pure in life and thought. The sodalities also served to confirm boys in the notion that family life was the ideal to which they should aspire and that within the ideal family there was a clear division of work, with the men providing the material resources and the women being the primary spiritual guardians within the home.

Finally, certain feminization processes were in operation in the education of boys which were aimed at developing their emotional commitment to family life; processes which had few parallels outside of the Catholic tradition. Christ, St. Paul and the medieval knight were often given as models of men who combined strength with gentleness and sensitivity, while the lives of the female saints were studied. The constant urging that boys consider whether they had a religious vocation was also significant as this meant that the 'caring' professions, and particularly teaching, were regularly eulogized for them at a time when such professions were coming to be seen as women's work by the rest of society. Furthermore, the Jesuits in particular tried to balance the emphasis on sport by encouraging music and drama, and this when the performing arts were tending to become the preserve of females in many other schools in the English-speaking world.[49]

In summary, the overall aim of Catholic education, regardless of the country concerned, has always been the preparation of students for a fuller life in eternity. During the period 1922–65 such preparation was interpreted largely to mean receiving instruction in religious dogma and following the Church's rules. Closely related to this was the emphasis placed on particular gender roles on the grounds that they constituted those roles best suited to ensuring the salvation of 'the faithful'. The part played by Catholic schools in Australia in responding to this emphasis was the subject matter of this chapter. Chapter 6 will now examine the fourth distinctive feature of the process of education in Catholic schools in Australia from 1922 to 1965; namely, the Irish influence.

Notes

[1] The Brigidine Sisters, *Directory of the Brigidine Sisters* (New South Wales, Australia: The Brigidine Sisters, 1955), p. 51.

[2] Sisters of Saint Joseph of the Most Sacred Heart of Jesus, *Customs and Practices of the Sisters of St. Joseph of the Most Sacred Heart of Jesus*, p. 9.

[3] The Christian Brothers, *Directory and Rules of the Congregation of the Brothers of the Christian Schools of Ireland*, p. 328.

[4] Ibid., p. 328.

[5] The Brigidine Sisters, *Directory of the Brigidine Sisters*, p. 1.

[6] The Sisters of Mercy, *Constitutions of the Congregation of the Australian Union of the Sisters of Our Lady of Mercy* (Canberra, Australia: The Sisters of Mercy—General Motherhouse, 1960), p. 3.

[7] S. Kennedy, *Faith and Feminism: Catholic Women's Struggle for Self-Expression* (Sydney: Studies in the Christian Movement, 1985), p. xv.

[8] A. Henderson, *Mary MacKillop's Sisters: A Life Unveiled* (Sydney: Harper-Collins, 1997), p. 10.

[9] K. Massam, *Sacred Threads: Catholic Spirituality in Australia 1922–1962*, p. 28.

[10] The Sisters of Saint Joseph of the Most Sacred Heart of Jesus, *My Yoke Is Sweet* (North Sydney, Australia: The Sisters of Saint Joseph of the Most Sacred Heart of Jesus, 1948).

[11] Ibid.

[12] Congregations of Religious Women in Western Australia, *In Search of the Promise of Something Special: Life with a Purpose* (Perth, Australia: Congregations of Religious Women in Western Australia, nd).

[13] Ibid.

[14] Sisters of Mercy, *Someone Just Like You* (recruitment pamphlet).

[15] Sisters of Our Lady of the Missions, *You Did Not Chose Me: No, I Chose You* (Perth: Sisters of Our Lady of the Missions, nd).

[16] The Sisters of Saint Joseph of the Most Sacred Heart of Jesus, *My Yoke Is Sweet*, p. 2.

[17] S. Kennedy, *Faith and Feminism: Catholic Women's Struggle for Self-Expression*, p. xii.

[18] The Sisters of Saint Joseph of the Most Sacred Heart of Jesus, *My Yoke Is Sweet*, p. 3.

[19] Ibid.

[20] IBVM, *Rules IBVM* (Dublin: IBVM, 1914), p. 9.

[21] J. West, *Daughters of Freedom* (Sutherland, NSW, Australia: Albatross Books, 1997), p. 25.

[22] In fact members of religious orders were expressly forbidden to discuss community life with 'seculars'. See The Brigidine Sisters, *Directory of the Brigidine Sisters*, p. 1. Here it is decreed that "the Sisters shall never make known to the children the private affairs of Community life, their own, or those of their Religious Sisters, and beware especially of showing disapprobation of the arrangements of Superiors that affect themselves or others".

[23] E. Leen, CSSp, *What is Education* (London: Burns, Oates and Washbourne, 1943).

24   The Brigidine Sisters, *Directory of the Brigidine Sisters*, p. 54.

25   J. West, *Daughters of Freedom*, p. 26.

26   Ibid.

27   Ibid., p. 32.

28   Ibid., p. 34.

29   K. Nelson and D. Nelson, *Sweet Mothers, Sweet Maids* (Ringwood, Victoria, Australia: Penguin Books, 1986), p. x.

30   See S. Burley, 'Resurrecting the religious experience of Catholic girls' schooling in South Australia in the 1920s', Proceedings of the ANZHES Annual Conference, Auckland, New Zealand, 1998.

31   K. Massam, *Sacred Threads: Catholic Spirituality in Australia 1922–1962*, p. 83.

32   S. Kennedy, *Faith and Feminism: Catholic Women's Struggle for Self-Expression*, p. x.

33   Pope Pius XI, *The Christian Education of Youth* (London: Catholic Truth Society, 1970).

34   B. Coldrey, 'A most unenviable reputation: the Christian Brothers and school discipline over two centuries,' *History of Education*, Vol. 21, No. 3, 1992, p. 283.

35   B. Oakley, 'Years of sawdust: the crack of the whip', *The Secondary Teacher*, Feb. 1967, p. 13.

36   B. Coldrey, 'A most unenviable reputation: the Christian Brothers and school discipline over two centuries', p. 283.

37   L. Clancy, *The Collapsible Man* (Melbourne: Outback Press, 1975), p. 55.

38   D. O'Grady, *Deschooling Kevin Carew* (Melbourne: Wren, 1974), p. 15.

39   K. Koch, *The Doubleman* (London: Angus and Robertson, 1955), p. 38.

40   Hawke has also recalled corporal punishment being administered in the girls' school she attended. See V. Hawke, 'Treaties and bargains with God', in K. Nelson and D. Nelson (eds.), *Sweet Mothers, Sweet Maids*, p. 9.

41   I. Brice, 'Ethnic masculinities in Australian boys' schools—Scots and Irish secondary schools in late nineteenth century Australia', Proceedings of the ISCHE Annual Conference, Sydney, Australia, 1998.

42   R. W. Connell, *Masculinities* (London: Polity Press, 1995).

43   I. Brice, 'Ethnic masculinities in Australian boys' schools—Scots and Irish secondary schools in late nineteenth century Australia'.

44   Ibid.

45   Ibid.

46   M. Scott, 'Masculinities and national identity in Adelaide boys' secondary schools, 1880–1911', Proceedings of the ANZHES Annual Conference, Auckland, New Zealand, 1998.

47   Concilium Legionis Mariae, *The Official Handbook of the Legion of Mary* (Dublin: The Legion of Mary, 1969), p. 4.

48   J. Hamilton, 'Faith and Football: Masculinities at Christian Brothers' College, Wakefield Street, 1879-1912' (unpublished M.Ed. thesis, The University of Adelaide, 2000), p. 164.

49   See D. Strong, *Jesuits in Australia* (Richmond, Victoria, Australia: Aurora Books, 1995), p. 391.

Chapter Six

A Strong Irish Influence in the Schools

Throughout the nineteenth century the great majority of Catholics in Australia were Irish-born or of Irish descent. After Federation in 1901 this situation slowly began to change as Irish migration to Australia declined while the number of Catholics from various parts of the rest of Europe slowly increased. Consequently, during the period 1922–65 the Catholic Church in Australia became more diverse with each passing year. Nevertheless, as this chapter argues, a very strong Irish influence continued to prevail.

The chapter is divided into three parts. First, the correspondence between Australian Catholicism and Irish Catholicism is treated briefly, the argument being that it was the particular Irish version of the religion which prevailed in Australian schools during the period 1922–65. The chapter then considers how, despite their declining numbers, Irish nuns, brothers and priests continued to have a significant presence in the schools during the period, thus ensuring that models of Catholicism other than their own made no inroads amongst 'the faithful'. Finally, attention is paid to the extent to which the presence of these Irish nuns, brothers and priests also helped to perpetuate a notion that it was Ireland rather than Britain which constituted 'the mother country' for Australian Catholics.

Australian Catholicism as Irish Catholicism

During the early convict period the Irish constituted about one-quarter of the entire population of Australia.[1] The real surge in Irish migration came during the Australian gold rush of the early 1850s when an estimated 84,000 arrived.[2] Around 80 per cent of this number stayed on to become permanent settlers. From the 1880s onwards the proportion of Irish-born in Australia, both as a percentage of foreign born and of the total population of the country, began to decline. The extent of the decline between then and 1971 has been represented as follows:

Table 6.1: Proportion of Irish-born in Australia between 1881 and 1971

Year	Irish-born	% of total population	% of foreign-born
1881	214,771	9.5	26.0
1891	229,156	7.2	22.7
1901	188,807	4.9	21.6
1911	141,331	3.2	18.5
1921	106,274	2.0	12.6
1931	79,185	1.2	8.8
1941	45,066	0.6	6.1
1951	47,844	0.5	3.7
1961	50,327	0.5	2.8

Source: D. H. Akenson, *The Irish Diaspora—A Primer*, p. 102.

Yet there was not a corresponding decline in Irish influence in the country. This is not difficult to comprehend; if one accepts that a definition of ethnicity can be based on one's place of birth or on that of one's ancestors, the extent of the early Irish migration to Australia ensured that the Irish have continued to be a very significant ethnic minority right up to the present day. On this, the following statistics on Irish ethnicity throughout the period 1861–1978 are instructive:

Table 6.2: Percentage of the Australian Population Between 1861 and 1978 Claiming Irish as Their Ethnic Background

1861	1891	1947	1978
25.5%	25.7%	23.0%	17.9%

Source: D. H. Akenson, *The Irish Diaspora—A Primer*, p. 113.

Focusing on these statistics, Akenson has concluded that if one puts the Irish Catholics and Irish Protestants in two different categories, the Irish Catholics on their own were the second largest ethnic group in Australia over the period 1861–1978.[3]

Given the situation described so far, it is not surprising that from about the middle of the 1850s Australian Catholicism was seen as being synonymous with Irish Catholicism. Prior to this, there was the possibility that the dominant model of the Church in Australia would have ended up being that of the English Benedictines. The first Catholic bishop in Australia was the Benedictine, John Bede Polding, who dreamt of civilizing and converting the country through establishing monasteries in which scholarship and Gregorian chant would prevail. The English Benedictines, however, could not provide Polding with sufficient priests. Consequently, diocesan clergy had to be sought to serve and to rule as bishops and pastors. The void was filled by priests from the Catholic Church in Ireland. By 1880 just one of the Irish seminaries alone, All Hallows, supplied half of the clergy in Australia.[4]

O'Farrell has aptly depicted the Irish style of Catholicism which came to prominence in Australia and which was taught and reinforced for so long in the schools as being clerical, authoritarian and non-intellectual.[5] Focusing specifically on the authoritarian dimension, Campion has summarized the situation as follows:

> Irish religion in Australia was a religion of law. There were laws about everything: laws about Lenten observance and laws about receiving Communion at Eastertime; laws about who could wash the altar linen and who could not; laws forbidding priests to stay out late at night; laws forbidding them to frequent theatres or racecourses or prize fights; laws forbidding them to join political parties, or read un-Catholic papers, or become guardians or tutors; and, of course, laws ordering what they must wear. It was a system of law and obedience was a prime virtue.[6]

The Irish Catholic clergy also brought with them to Australia such religious practices as the Forty Hours' Adoration, novenas, devotion to the Sacred Heart, and various male and female lay sodalities. They put an enormous effort into raising funds to construct churches and cathedrals. As the next section of this chapter demonstrates, certain

Irish influences in the schools played a part in ensuring that Irish Catholicism remained the dominant model of Catholicism in Australia long after the Catholic population ceased to be first-generation Irish; so much so that it has been concluded that it was not until the late 1960s that "the descendants of the Irish in Australia became sufficiently free of the authoritarian seriousness of their heritage to be able to poke fun at it".[7]

The Perpetuation of Irish Catholicism Amongst Future Generations through the Continuing Presence of Irish Nuns, Brothers and Priests in the Schools

For nearly a hundred years, the Irish Catholic hierarchy was able to influence the choice of bishops for Australia and ensure that the vast majority of them were Irish.[8] It has already been pointed out that Irish priests continued to dominate the diocesan clergy long after the Catholic population ceased to be first-born Irish.[9] These diocesan priests perpetuated an Irish version of the Church in Australia, with its particular worldview, while the great majority of the rest of the diocesan clergy, being Australian, were products of homes and schools where no alternative models of the Church and of Catholic ideas and practices were presented to them.

The number of Irish religious in the classrooms, particularly Irish nuns, was most significant. A statistical survey of religious personnel in the late 1970s calculated that over the course of a hundred years around two thousand Irish girls had come to Australia to join religious orders; nearly fifteen hundred of them were still at work or in convents throughout the country in 1976.[10] This is not to ignore the fact that between 1910 and 1940 there was a shift such that the majority of nuns in Australia became predominantly Australian-born.[11] Nevertheless, further recruitment from Ireland by a number of congregations right through to the 1960s continued to be successful, thus ensuring the continuation of a strong Irish presence in the schools and, consequently, an Irish ethos.

The presence of Irish nuns, religious brothers and priests in Australia reflected a trend that continued from the latter half of the nineteenth century—that of the Church expanding internationally. Fahey[12] comments that the Catholic Church, from its European base, built up a powerful position in North America and Oceania, made substantial inroads into Africa and expanded its bridgeheads in China, India, Japan and other Asian countries. Specifically with regard to Ireland's contribution to this movement, he states:

> The Irish church was a notable force in this international expansion of Catholicism. It retained a strong sense of its membership of an international ecclesiastical community not just because of its allegiance to Rome, but also because of the 'spiritual empire' which its floods of emigrant priests, religious and laity had fashioned around the world.[13]

Indeed, the Catholic Church in Ireland became the second largest *per capita* contributor of missionaries in the Catholic Church in the first half of the twentieth century, Holland being the largest.[14]

Most of the religious who came from Ireland to teach in Australia during the period 1922–65 were nuns. The forces which brought this about, in addition to a strong religious motivation in many cases, were much the same as those which resulted in much greater numbers being recruited in Ireland to work in convents elsewhere, particularly Africa, as well as those which led to great numbers of lay people leaving the country. In particular, it must be remembered that Irish society had, since the middle of the nineteenth century, been preparing its youth for emigration in order to maintain the existing social structure favoring middle-class dominance and to ensure that the population never returned to the precariously high levels which contributed to the Great Famine of 1845–48.[15] Coupled with this was the contraction in opportunities for women in Catholic-dominated Ireland after independence in 1922.[16]

For some women, emigration to a convent offered more security than was to be had from joining the workforce in Britain or the United States. When priests, religious brothers or nuns returned on holidays they raised some attractive possibilities. On this a sister of

the order of Saint Joseph of the Most Sacred Heart of Jesus has
commented as follows:

> In the church we would see people who had come home from missionary
> countries. There would be nuns and brothers and priests. There was always
> that colourful tone about our holidays. And we were intrigued because nuns
> did not teach us. We went to the national school [government primary
> school]. There were religion classes but our faith came more from home. It
> was part and parcel of it. And when we saw these garbed people we thought
> they were absolutely magnificent.[17]

Many girls considering emigrating to become a nun were also attracted
by the fact that they had aunts, sisters or cousins in convents
overseas, including Australia, who would ensure their well-being on
arrival.

Various religious orders regularly sought recruits through
advertisements in the Catholic newspapers in Ireland, through
pamphlets distributed to schools, and through journals like the *Irish
Catholic Directory*. Girls "animated by the missionary spirit and
vocation" who wanted "to consecrate their lives to God" were
encouraged to join so that they could "devote their lives to the
conversion and uplifting of pagan women" and "promote the greatest
of works, the salvation of souls".[18] The nature of the work was
portrayed as being not only heroic, but also very extensive and very
successful. The following is representative of the type of
advertisements posted:

> Young Irish priests and nuns have died for the Faith in West Africa. To that
> sacrifice which was Calvary's own, coupled with charity from Ireland, is
> attributed the great development of the six great Irish missions in Liberia,
> Benin Coast, Western Nigeria, Kaduna, Jos and Ondo-Ilorin.[19]

Those who came to Australia frequently recall that they were
attracted by the notion of educating Aboriginal children. Most found,
however, that when they commenced teaching the faces in the desks
were as white as those they knew in Ireland.

Irish girls who came to Australia as nuns were also recruited
through a variety of other routes. Some came through the
encouragement of local priests in Ireland who had connections with

religious orders. One nun who joined the Sisters of Saint Joseph of the Most Sacred Heart of Jesus has characterized as follows how the processes operated in her case:

> I was one of seven children reared by my father after my mother died when I was three. I remember meeting a Carmelite priest while on a Children of Mary Sodality retreat in Kilkenny in 1925; he mentioned the Sisters of St. Joseph in Australia. The sister in charge of the sodality was sceptical about advising young girls to leave Ireland for the unknown in distant countries. She wrote to her Jesuit brother in Australia for information and he assured her: 'Send as many as you can to the Sisters of St. Joseph in Australia'.[20]

Another nun who joined the same order has recalled, in a similar vein:

> [I] was shopping with my cousin, Mary Murphy, in Glenduff, Ireland, when we met a Miss Reynolds who greeted us with: 'Now you're the kind of girls Fr. Edward Carroll is hoping to meet, to go to Australia'. That started us thinking and, another cousin, Mida Dwane, was very interested. A few months later, ten girls decided with us to leave for Australia to join the Sisters of St. Joseph at North Sydney. My mother was a saintly woman and had wanted to be a nun herself. She feared I'd be living among primitive people in Australia, but my father, who had a sister, Helen, in a convent in Australia, was pleased that I decided to do the same.[21]

Others were recruited by a variety of religious orders through St. Brigid's Missionary College in Callan. This special juniorate was established in 1884 and continued to function until 1959. It enrolled girls who had completed primary school and who showed a desire to join a religious order and work overseas. It was, in fact, a school for future nuns. In its seventy-five years of existence approximately two thousand girls attended this kind of 'pre-novitiate'.[22]

St. Brigid's Missionary College was run by the Sisters of Mercy, but any order wishing to recruit girls for overseas work was able to approach its students. Other orders ran similar juniorates or secondary boarding schools for those aspiring to work on 'the missions' with their own order.[23] The Sisters of Saint Joseph of the Most Sacred Heart of Jesus had one such juniorate, St. Joseph's, at Newmarket, County Cork. This secondary boarding school was established in 1927 for the reception and education of candidates for the order in Australia and had both Irish and Australian sisters on staff. From then until 1973, Newmarket, according to one official historian of the order, "became a bountiful source of volunteers for the Sydney Josephite novitiate".[24] This historian goes on to give the following summary of the numbers who came to Australia from Newmarket over the years:

> Twenty-five candidates reached Sydney in 1928, followed by 19 in 1929, thence an annual group till the outbreak of World War 2. Between 1947 and 1950, at least three small groups migrated, bringing professed members who had completed the novitiate in Newmarket during the war, and new candidates. In the 1950s there was a steady flow of candidates till 1959, when no group came, as the candidates were considered too young. Numbers dropped in the 1960s, reflecting a pattern in novitiates in Western society. In 1971 the congregational chapter decided to close Newmarket and its Sydney juniorate.[25]

A common theme binding together girls who went to St. Joseph's, Newmarket, and subsequently went to Australia to join the Sisters of Saint Joseph of the Most Sacred Heart of Jesus was that they were from fairly humble backgrounds and, consequently, were attracted by the fact that the order did not have lay sisters and did not require a dowry of those who joined. They were usually recruited for the school by nuns from the order visiting the senior grades in local primary schools. These recruiting sisters first of all got the local bishop's permission to operate in his diocese. Then, with the further permission of the principals of the primary schools, they spoke to young girls about 'responding to God's call' to work in Australia.

Some orders, like the Dominican Sisters and the Loreto Sisters, sent professed nuns to Australia, while others recruited girls in Ireland, who then left the country to become postulants in Australia. Others yet again did their preliminary religious training in postulancies in Ireland before emigrating to complete it in Australia. Amongst those religious orders who had postulancies in Ireland for girls who would go to Australia for the remainder of their religious training and subsequent work were the Sisters of Saint John of God at Ballinamore Convent, Kiltimagh, County Mayo, servicing Western Australia, and the Sisters of Mercy, Timoleague, County Cork, servicing the Archdiocese of Brisbane. A number of novitiates were also run in

Ireland specifically to prepare girls up to the stage of taking final religious vows before going abroad. Amongst these was the novitiate of the Congregation of the Daughters of Our Lady of the Sacred Heart at Glandore in County Cork. This order had missions in the Pacific Islands, The East Indies, Australia, Africa and South America.

The continuing drive to recruit Irish girls to join religious orders in Australia succeeded to such an extent that it ensured not only a significant minority of Irish-born nuns in the larger centers of population, but also an often near majority of Irish nuns in more sparsely populated regions.[26] Also, throughout the country a very large proportion of Australian nuns in all of the orders came from suburbs or country areas of fairly concentrated Irish settlement. Furthermore, a number of orders, despite their majority Australian-born membership, continued, particularly up to the 1940s, to return Irish women as their major superiors. Notable examples in this regard were the large Brisbane Congregation of the Mercy Order and the largest amalgamation of Presentation congregations of the order in the country, the Victorian amalgamation. In this way, branches of religious orders were able to ensure a continuation of an Irish model of religious formation in their convents.

While the number of Irish-born Christian Brothers had become a minority in Australia during the period under consideration, Coldrey[27] has noted that the Irish influence continued to be very strong. This was due to the order being centralized, with the Superior General being Irish and based in Dublin, and with the distinctive training structure for the Brothers in Australia being overseen for many years by Irish-born members who had themselves been trained in Ireland. In particular, Coldrey mentions Br. P. J. Barron who, between 1895 and 1935, moulded the order in Australia "to his own image and likeness".[28] Barron brought with him from Ireland an obsession with success in public examinations because of the prestige and status which it had brought to the schools in Ireland, and he instilled a similar obsession amongst the Christian Brothers in Australia. In this, he promoted an anti-intellectualism in the order, where the emphasis was on constant hard work aimed at learning what was necessary to do well in examinations and uncovering the rules of the examination 'game', rather than studying and promoting learning for the intrinsic good to be gained from intellectual development.

Overall, then, the continuing Irish presence amongst the teaching force in the classrooms perpetuated the Irish model of the Church through the schools. The influence of Irish-born teachers was reinforced by the great number of Australian-born nuns, brothers and priests who were also receptive to an Irish model of the Church. They felt this way because of their own Irish descent and the influence of the Irish members who continued to occupy positions of authority in their respective religious orders. With certain notable exceptions, this meant an anti-intellectualism and an authoritarianism. Equally, Christie and Smith have noted that it meant the adoption of an isolationist approach within Australian society:

> In various forms this period has been characterised by an isolationist or separatist attitude. Some of the reasons posited for this particular phenomenon have centred on the issue of social class and the lack of influence of Irish Catholics and clergy until the post World War 2 period. O'Farrell (1977), in looking at this period, has described in great detail the way in which a dogmatic church, clerically led, was forced to defend itself against what it perceived as an error-ridden, hostile world. Other factors identified as influencing the general attitudes of Catholics have been such things as the perceived influence of freemasonry, the Irish question, conscription and the influence of fundamentalist Protestant societies that flourished in Australia from time to time.[29]

The dominant attitude which prevailed contributed to what O'Farrell has characterized as "a kind of residual disposition to acknowledge Irish origins and to feel most at home with things and people of Irish derivation".[30] Thus, various practices were carried out in the classroom, not only by the Irish-born, but also by a great many Australian-born nuns, brothers and priests, which ensured a perpetuation of a notion that it was Ireland rather than England which was the 'mother country' of Australian Catholics.

A Different 'Mother Country'

During the nineteenth century, Irish Catholics in Australia had turned to their Church to help them develop an identity of which they could be proud in the face of the alienation they experienced in the English colonies. Consequently, a very strong association developed between being Irish and being Catholic. This manifested itself in a variety of ways. Not only did the Catholic population build imposing churches, but they named them after Irish saints such as St. Brigid, St. Kevin, St. Declan, St. Canice, St. Columba, St. Columbkille, St. Brendan and St. Fiacra.[31] The feast days of these saints were celebrated with great pride and enthusiasm, and were given extensive reportage in Catholic newspapers. St. Patrick's Day occupied pride of place in the calendar of special Irish Church celebrations. In 1924, for example, the Archbishop of Sydney circulated "a Litany in honour of St. Patrick, to be recited after Mass on the three mornings before the feast of St. Patrick (100 days indulgence each time)".[32] In their reportage, Catholic newspapers made much of such special occasions, just as they did of the annual St. Patrick's Day masses and parades held in all of the major cities and country towns around Australia.

Other developments also served to impose on the minds of Australian Catholics that to be Irish and Catholic went hand-in-hand. The "mother church of Australian Catholicism, St. Mary's Cathedral in Sydney" is, as Campion reminds us, "significantly ringed with an iron fence of shamrocks; it contains not one, but two statues of St. Patrick; and its most beautiful altar is the altar of the Irish Saints".[33] Many of the early schools which were opened by the religious orders were named after Irish saints, most notably St. Patrick and St. Brigid. The schools continued on with those names into the twentieth century, thus maintaining their Irish connection.

The presence of Irish nuns, brothers and priests in Australian Catholic schools during the period 1922–65 also helped to perpetuate the nineteenth-century notion that it was Ireland rather than Britain which constituted 'the mother country' for Australian Catholics. Teachers were constantly reminded of the Christian-nationalist theme in Irish history; that of Ireland having been a 'land of saints and scholars' during its 'golden era' from the ninth to the twelfth century, when Irish missionaries Christianized Europe. Such reminders went as follows:

While Ireland received the Faith from one who was not an Irishman but a stranger, she made such extraordinary progress in sanctity and learning within an incredibly short period, that she became not only the home of Catholic faith and culture where strangers from every nation in Europe were welcomed in her Monastic Schools, but she sent her teachers all over Europe and even to Iceland. For four hundred years Ireland was literally the university of Europe. It was Irish monks who brought the Catholic Faith to England. It was Irish monks who taught the Saxon to read and write.[34]

This theme was, in turn, presented to students as an inheritance of which they should be proud and of which they should keep reminding themselves as a motivator in their studies. In various speeches given in schools by bishops, priests, brothers, nuns and prominent lay Catholics, a romantic image was painted of great Irish monasteries in the early Christian period as centers of learning, prayer and missionary work which were stocked with beautifully illuminated manuscripts and inhabited by devout and generous nuns and monks.

The notion of Ireland being the mother country for Australian Catholics was expressed in various textbooks used in the schools. Musgrave reminds us that the second of the *Catholic History Readers* used in Melbourne since the 1930s was entitled 'The Land of Our Fathers' and contained a section on 'Christian Ireland'.[35] Irish nuns, in particular, perpetuated this emphasis by infusing the curriculum with Irish themes. On this it is quite common to read reports along the following lines:

[Sister] Brendan loved teaching literature. Some critics thought most of primary school was drama and other such forms of literature. All her pupils knew about St. Brendan the Navigator. Each day they were taught an Irish poem or song.[36]

School newsletters, in recording the deaths of Irish nuns, also made much of the Australian Church's indebtedness to these women who, as it was regularly put, made a heroic sacrifice, supposedly leaving their families and their homelands to 'give their all' to Australia.

During the nineteenth century and the first two decades of the twentieth century the notion of Australian Catholicism coming from Irish Catholicism was accompanied by strong anti-English feeling. The Christian Brothers in Australia had a particular reputation in this regard. This is not surprising given that most of the brothers were still Irish-born and had been trained in Ireland where the order had been most prominent both in the Gaelic-revival movement and in the republican and separatist movements from the mid-1880s to Independence from Britain in 1922. In Australia they used their Irish texts, which were highly nationalistic and full of Irish-related material. Their *Irish History Reader* of 1916, for example, advised teachers to:

> Dwell with pride and in glowing terms on Ireland's glorious past...her devotion through the centuries to the Faith brought by her National Apostle...[Pupils] must be taught that Irishmen, claiming the right to make their own laws, should never rest content until their nation's Parliament is restored.[37]

The Irish were portrayed as being the oppressed, seeking freedom from English tyranny.

In the 1920s an edition of the Christian Brothers' readers suitable for the Australian scene was brought out which was devoid of such anti-British sentiment. While the occasional brother or nun was not beyond making remarks in the classroom about the atrocities committed by the 'Black and Tans' in the Irish War of Independence of 1919–21, the Irish Civil War of 1922 largely brought an end to anti-English feeling in Australia, with the great majority judging that the degree of independence granted to Ireland was just and fair. By the 1940s Catholics in Australia were quite clear that they were not Irish, but rather were of Irish Catholic descent. This found expression in school magazines in extracts like the following:

> We are not Irish. We are Australian and proud of it. But we know that a great part of the heritage of the Catholic Faith that we enjoy came to us from the Irish settlers who, for many of us, were our ancestors.[38]

Massam[39] also reminds us that school magazines cited a link between religion and civic duty. She recalls in particular the coronation of Queen Elizabeth in 1953 being celebrated in Catholic schools and the fact that during the royal visit in 1954 the Catholic press used banner headlines to welcome the monarch to Australia. Nevertheless, she concludes that "warm as the reception was, it was nonetheless issued as a separate, distinct and specifically Catholic demonstration of allegiance to the queen".[40]

In the Catholic schools pupils were now encouraged to think of themselves as part of an Australian nation which grew out of an Irish contribution, rather than of an Australia which was "an extension of Britain over the seas".[41] Arnold captures well the nationalist perspective presented on Irish history and the notion promoted that there was continuity between it and the experience of Catholics in Australia:

> We knew of the tyranny that had brought starvation and death during the potato blight, even while Irish food was being exported from Ireland to England. Above all, we knew about the hedge schools where forbidden learning of the faith took place. We were also aware that in Australia, Catholics had a hard time of it. The State tried to take our faith away from us ('Faith of our fathers, we will be true to thee till death', we sang in church) and the Masons tried to grind us down by denying us jobs. It was well known that certain public service departments encouraged Catholic advancement while in others it was impossible to 'get on'.[42]

At the same time, while this Irish element remained central in the notion presented to the Catholic school population of what it was to be an Australian, it had to concede some ground as the new migrants of the post-World War Two years began to slowly change the character of Australian Catholicism. This meant locating allegiance to Ireland as part of a broader allegiance to Rome, the spiritual home of most Australian Catholics. Thus, when the Catholic Education Office in Melbourne produced its graded *Catholic History Readers* in 1934, the view presented of the Catholic world was an international one. In particular, there was an emphasis on the background out of which Christianity grew, so that the Bible and Roman history were given prominence. The titles of the Catholic history readers show this international emphasis. The first, *The Kings of the Earth*, contained stories such as 'The East', on 'Greece and Rome' and on 'the Coming of Christ'. The second was called *Land of Our Fathers* and contained sections about Roman Britain, Christian England and the Northmen. The third, *The Victory of the Cross*, covered the late Roman Empire and the Dark Ages. There followed *The Story of the Middle Ages* and, lastly, *The Changing World*, which covered the Renaissance and the Reformation. These themes were supported by articles in *Children's World*, published by the Catholic Education Office in Melbourne eight times yearly in three graded issues from 1934 to 1965.

Throughout the period under consideration, Catholic schools put much less emphasis on the growth of Britain than did government and Protestant schools. Rather, they focused on the spread of Christianity and the development of the Catholic Church in Europe and its spread to Australia. Also, as Musgrave puts it:

> Children were invited to belong to the Australian body politic, but always within a religious and, particularly because the Roman Catholic Church was so international in focus, in a world setting...Loyalty to the Crown was offered as a duty of an Australian citizen, but the sovereign was of Australia and drew authority from God and his internationalist Church on Earth, not from a vaguely Anglican Parliament in London.[43]

At the same time, it needs to be kept in mind that Australian society in general began to experience a decline in "the influence of the British connection"[44] after World War Two. This decline was promoted not only by the new wave of immigrants, particularly from southern Europe, but also by the growth in influence of American companies on the Australian economy, particularly through the mass media.[45] The consequence was a more multi-cultural Australia, containing as one of its elements an Anglo-Celtic dimension which evolved from a closing of the gap between the traditional Irish Catholic and British Protestant traditions. This did not result in a dismantling of the Catholic education sector in Australia. What did eventuate, however, was that from around the middle of the 1960s the sector evolved in a manner which moved it far away from its Irish Catholic origins.

Notes

[1] D. H. Akenson, *The Irish Diaspora—A Primer* (Toronto: P. D. Meaney Company, Inc., 1996), p. 96.

[2] Ibid, p. 113.

[3] Ibid.

[4] P. O'Farrell, *The Catholic Church in Australia. A Short History: 1788–1967* (London: Geoffrey Chapman, 1969), p. 83.

[5] P. O'Farrell, *The Irish in Australia* (Kensington, NSW, Australia: New South Wales University Press, 1993).

[6] E. Campion, 'Irish religion in Australia', *The Australasian Catholic Record*, Vol. 55, 1978, p. 11.

[7] P. O'Farrell, *The Irish in Australia* (Kensington, NSW: New South Wales University Press, 1993), p. 301.

[8] P. O'Farrell, *The Catholic Church in Australia. A Short History: 1788–1967*.

[9] This can be illustrated for the Archdiocese of Perth, for example, as follows:

Table 6.3: Irish-born Diocesan Priests in the Archdiocese of Perth

Year	Total Number	Number Who Were Irish
1935–40	51	31
1955–60	172	81
1960–65	209	97

Source: Archives of the Archdiocese of Perth

[10] M. R. MacGinley, *A Dynamic of Hope: Institutes of Women Religious in Australia*, pp. 288–290.

[11] Ibid, p. 289.

[12] T. Fahey, 'Catholicism and industrial society in Ireland', in J. H. Goldthorpe and C T. Whelan (eds.), *The Development of Industrial Society in Ireland* (Oxford: Oxford University Press, 1994), p. 247.

[13] Ibid.

[14] P. J. Duffy, *The Lay Teacher* (Dublin: Fallons, 1967), p. 3.

[15] T. Inglis, *Moral Monopoly: The Rise and Fall of the Catholic Church in Modern Ireland* (Dublin: University College Dublin Press, 1998), pp. 196–199.

[16] See L. O'Dowd, 'Church, state and women: The aftermath of partition', in C. Curtin, P. Jackson and B. O'Connor (eds.), *Gender in Irish Society* (Galway, Ireland: Officina Typographica, 1987), pp. 3–36.

[17] A. Henderson, *Mary MacKillop's Sisters: A Life Unveiled* (Sydney: Harper-Collins, 1997), p. 62.

[18] This is representative of the type of language used in advertisements appearing in the *Irish Catholic Directory and Almanac* published annually in Dublin by James Duffy and Company, Ltd.

[19] *Irish Catholic Directory and Almanac* (Dublin: James Duffy and Company Ltd., 1940), p. 259.

[20] K. E. Burford, *Unfurrowed Fields. A Josephite Story NSW 1872–1972* (Sydney: St. Joseph's Convent, 1991), p. 139.

[21] Ibid.

[22] St. Brigid's College, *St Brigid's College Callan Golden Jubilee Book 1999* (Callan, Ireland: St. Brigid's College, 1999), p. 3.

[23] These included the following: the juniorate of the Sisters of St. Joseph of Cluny, Ferbane, County Offally; the juniorate of the Daughters of Mercy and Joseph

(Ladies of Mercy) at Castlecar, County Offaly; the juniorate at Immaculata Convent, Mallow, County Cork; the juniorate of the Daughters of the Cross, Donaghmore, County Tyrone; the juniorate of the Incarnate Word Convent, Dunmore, County Galway; and the juniorate of the Sisters Servants of the Holy Ghost and Mary Immaculate, Mountbellew, County Galway.

[24] J. Tranter, 'The religious dimension of an Australian religious sisterhood: the Sisters of St. Joseph', in P. O'Sullivan (ed), *Religion and Identity* (London: Leicester University Press, 1996), p. 248.

[25] Ibid.

[26] The situation in the Archdiocese of Perth, for example, provides a good example of the latter pattern:

Table 6.4: Religious Sisters in Congregations of Nuns Involved Primarily in Teaching in the Archdiocese of Perth

Year: Total No. of Sisters in WA		Total No. of Sisters Who Were Irish
1935	591	248
1960	760	245
1965	740	236

Source: Archives of the Archdiocese of Perth.

When these numbers are broken down for those religious orders with the largest number of nuns involved in education in the Archdiocese which also happened to be heavily Irish-influenced, the pattern for the years 1935, 1950 and 1965 was as follows:

Year: 1935	Total Number	Number Who Were Irish
Mercy Sisters	303	158
Presentation Sisters	43	36
St. Joseph of the Apparition	73	19
St. Joseph of the Sacred Heart	45	16
Year: 1950	**Total Number**	**Number Who Were Irish**
Mercy Sisters	326	143
Presentation Sisters	56	27
St. Joseph of the Apparition	103	34
St. Joseph of the Sacred Heart	90	30
Year: 1965	**Total Number**	**Number Who Were Irish**
Mercy Sisters	340	125
Presentation Sisters	53	32
St. Joseph of the Apparition	90	24
St. Joseph of the Sacred Heart	71	22

A similar pattern existed in certain other parts of the country. For example, the percentage of those who joined the Mercy Order in the Diocese of Townsville and in the Vicariate of Cooktown over the same period were in the region of 50 per cent and 30 per cent Irish-born, respectively.

[27] B. Coldrey, 'The influence of Irish traditions on the policies and professional training of the Christian Brothers in Victoria, 1868–1930 (unpublished M.Ed. thesis, The University of Melbourne, 1973), pp.156-165.

[28] Ibid., p. 158.

[29] D. Christie, and P. Smith, 'Teachers' careers in Catholic schools', in R. MacClean and P. McKenzie (eds.), *Australian Teachers' Careers* (Hawthorn, Victoria, Australia: Australian Council for Educational Research, 1991), p. 214.

[30] P. O'Farrell. *The Catholic Church in Australia. A Short History: 1788–1967* (London: Geoffrey Chapman, 1969), p. 158.

[31] E. Campion, 'Irish religion in Australia', *The Australasian Catholic Record*, Vol. 55, 1978, p. 10.

[32] Ibid.

[33] Ibid.

[34] S. M. Hogan, 'A crusade for vocations to the teaching orders', in Australian Catholic Education Congress, *Australian Catholic Education Congress, Adelaide, Australia* (Melbourne: The Advocate Press, 1937), p. 151.

[35] P. W. Musgrave, 'To be an Australian? Secular and Catholic versions of national identity in primary school textbooks, 1895–1964', p. 29.

[36] A. McLay, *Women Out of Their Sphere* (Perth, WA, Australia: Vanguard Press, 1992), p. 299.

[37] P. W. Musgrave, 'To be an Australian? Secular and Catholic versions of national identity in primary school textbooks, 1895–1964', p. 31.

[38] Ibid.

[39] K. Massam, *Sacred Threads: Catholic Spirituality in Australia 1922–1962*, p. 35.

[40] Ibid.

[41] P. W. Musgrave, 'To be an Australian? Secular and Catholic versions of national identity in primary school textbooks, 1895–1964', p. 36.

[42] J. Arnold, *Mother Superior Mother Inferior*, p. 78.

[43] P. W. Musgrave, 'To be an Australian? Secular and Catholic versions of national identity in primary school textbooks, 1895–1964', p. 31.

[44] P. W. Musgrave, *Society and the Curriculum in Australia* (Sydney: George Allen and Unwin, 1979), p. 145.

[45] Ibid., p. 145.

Chapter Seven

Analysis and Conclusion

King has noted that a strong centralizing tendency was manifest in the Roman Empire before Christ, and that "in the Roman Catholic Church which has shaped so much of Christendom a centralized and hierarchical form of administration was perpetuated".[1] During the nineteenth century the Catholic Church strengthened this administrative approach. In doing so, it was responding to attacks which owed their origins to its previously privileged position in several continental countries, most notably France and Italy. The new conservative and dogmatic ideology underpinning this response, which achieved ascendancy within European Catholicism, was termed 'Ultramontanism' by contemporaries. It was a major influence shaping three of the features which characterized the process of education in Catholic schools in many countries during the latter half of the nineteenth and the first half of the twentieth century: the fact that it was conducted within an authoritarian framework; the major emphasis placed on religious instruction and on ensuring that schooling had an all-pervasive religious atmosphere; and the promotion of particular gender roles.

In Australia, these features took on a very strict and oppressive form during the period 1922–65. The key to understanding this is to be found in the additional feature which characterized the process of education in Catholic schools in the country, namely, the Irish influence. This Irish influence, which was discussed in Chapter 6, as already demonstrated, was a distinct feature in its own right. Also, however, a particular Irish version of Catholicism strongly impregnated the other three features. Thus, the origins of this 'Irish Catholicism' need to be appreciated in order to develop an understanding of Australian Catholicism and the processes of education in Australian Catholic schools up to the mid-1960s.

It is true that Ireland has a long history of being a Catholic country and that it maintained its Catholicism during the Reformation. Yet, the version of Irish Catholicism which has come to be associated with an austere, authoritarian and puritanical outlook on life does not have the long and glorious history which many have come to assume. During much of the eighteenth century a high level of religious practice was not characteristic of "the Irish masses",[2] the traditional Gaelic-speaking peasantry. By the beginning of the nineteenth century, however, an English-speaking Irish Catholic middle class of professionals, well-off farmers and commercial families had come into prominence alongside 'the masses' and was readying itself to take the place of the old Protestant ruling class. Part of the process of defining itself as an elite was "the business of creating and maintaining a well-defined and well-ordered modern class system within the Catholic community".[3] The religious orders played a major part in this process. In their approach to their work they argued for the need to educate the poor and prepare them as best they could for the "humble state in life to which it has pleased God to call them".[4] In other words, they sought to supplant Catholic Gaelic culture, with its "complex web of archaic beliefs and practices of a magical or naturalistic kind"[5] by instilling new feelings of piety amongst the poor, thus shaping and reinforcing class divisions. Their most extensive project involved the establishment of schools for the religious and secular education of children.

Also around the turn of the nineteenth century, French Jansenistic-type ideas began to infiltrate the Catholic Church in Ireland through the national seminary, St. Patrick's College, Maynooth. Some have argued that the particular influence should more accurately be termed 'Rigorism' or 'Augustinianism'.[6] Notwithstanding these distinctions, scholars are in general agreement that the discipline and doctrines taught at Maynooth were "of a kind calculated to foster the most severe moral attitudes and puritanical outlook on life in general".[7] What was stressed was the sinfulness of human beings and "the innate corruption of human nature",[8] with an emphasis on dealing with this human condition through "a systematic discipline, surveillance and sexualisation of the body".[9]

Between 1845 and 1848, the marginal class in Irish society was devastated by the failure of the potato crop. The new civilizing role of the religious orders, coupled with the Jansenistic inclinations of the diocesan clergy, now converged to become the dominant world view in Irish society. This world view served to legitimize the activities of those in the middle class as they set about imposing their own values on society; values which, as Lee has put it, "sanctified the primacy of property in the rural status system".[10] The continuing practice of emigration, particularly to the United States, Britain and Australia, served as a 'safety valve' for dealing with any surplus population which might have constituted a threat to middle-class ascendancy. The 'cloister' was the other great safety valve; even though the overall Catholic population of Ireland fell by 27 per cent between 1861 and 1901, there was, at the same time, an increase of 137 per cent in the number of priests, monks and nuns.[11]

The convergence of clerical and lay standards of sexual behavior at this time is particularly striking. Jansenistic and puritanical attitudes to sex outside of marriage characterized the great majority of the Irish Catholic clergy after the Great Famine. These attitudes, in turn, reflected those of the new "hard, calculating, materialistic society"[12] where "rigid patterns of inheritance, combined with a demographic regime that demanded that large numbers of men and women married only very late or not at all"[13] made a very strict code of sexual behavior essential. Priests' personal conduct was equally strictly controlled by a tightening of regulations forbidding them to hunt, to attend theatres and to drink in public, while "their growing separation from the laity was symbolised by the adoption for the first time of a distinctive clerical dress".[14]

From the middle of the nineteenth century the Irish Catholic Church also became characterized by a clerically dominated hierarchical organization. This reflected the approach of the Church internationally; an approach which has been aptly summarized as follows:

By the mid-nineteenth century Catholicism throughout Europe was reacting to the challenge of an increasingly pluralist and rationalistic society by a vigorous assertion of its exclusive claims to truth and authority. The Syllabus of Errors (1864), the determined defence of the Pope's temporal possessions against the movement for Italian unification, and the proclamation of papal infallibility (1870), were all reflections of this mood of intransigent defiance in the face of a hostile world.[15]

A major consequence in Ireland of the adoption of a particular branch of the ideology underpinning this approach was the reshaping of popular religious practice. The new pattern which had emerged by about the 1860s has been described thus:

[A]ttendance at Sunday mass for the first time became almost universal, while confession and communion became more regular and more frequent. The same period saw the widespread dissemination of a range of auxiliary services—benediction, stations of the cross, novenas, processions and retreats—as well as the routine use of scapulars, medals, religious images and other aids to private devotion. Individual religious practice was encouraged and regimented through the proliferation of lay confraternities and sodalities. Meanwhile the psychological impact of Catholic religious worship was increased by a transformation of its physical setting, as new or improved church buildings, more elaborate vestments and lavish altar furnishings allowed services to be conducted with a new emphasis on external magnificence and display.[16]

The result of the great effort put into popular religious renewal was a population "moulded into a thoroughly sacramental and Mass-going Church".[17] This population, in turn, provided sufficient numbers of nuns, brothers and priests to assist in the spread of the Catholic Church and the 'new Catholicism' throughout much of the British Empire, including Australia.

Given the scenario painted so far, the reports of an undisciplined Irish Catholic clergy and laity in the early years of colonization in Australia can be attributed to their arrival in pre-famine days and being representative possibly of the earlier version of Irish Catholicism associated with the then strong Gaelic cultural tradition. By contrast, when bishops, priests, religious brothers and nuns began coming to Australia in large numbers from the 1850s onwards, they were representative of the new Irish Catholicism. Furthermore, they administered to a predominantly English-speaking population which had emigrated largely from that part of Ireland where the new 'legalistic' version of Catholicism had been in operation for the longest period of time and where it had its greatest success; namely, counties Tipperary, Limerick, Clare and Kilkenny.[18]

The clergy, both diocesan and those who belonged to religious orders, played a major part in ensuring that the new form of Catholicism was maintained amongst those who emigrated to Australia. The establishment of schools was crucial in this task. By the middle of the nineteenth century, Catholic schools, along with schools of the other churches, had been provided in all of the Australian colonies, albeit in a somewhat haphazard fashion. The Church enunciated strongly its position that, wherever possible, Catholic parents should send their children to Catholic schools and that in doing so they should not suffer undue financial disadvantage. Initially, there was some satisfaction with the situation whereby grants were made to religious societies to assist in paying teachers' salaries and the cost of school buildings. Nevertheless, sectarian bitterness arose for a number of reasons. In particular, the privileged position conferred on the Church of England by the civil authorities was opposed by the Catholic Church.[19]

New South Wales attempted to come up with a reasonable solution when, during the 1850s, it instituted a 'dual' system.[20] Under this system, a Board of Denominational Education provided government aid for schools of the various denominations. At the same time, a Board of National Education was given the responsibility of establishing a system of state-controlled non-denominational schools. Other colonies followed a similar route. Such arrangements came to an end between 1872 and 1893 when all colonies passed education acts leading to the establishment of government-controlled school systems and the withdrawal of state aid to church schools. The Protestant churches reluctantly accepted this development and began to concentrate very much on running their elite fee-paying grammar schools. The Catholic Church protested vehemently, but its efforts were to no avail.

A fairly definite pattern of educational provision emerged after the passing of the education acts. White has characterized this as follows:

The schools of the colonial elite were private and Protestant, and looked towards Britain; the schools of the Irish-Australians were poor and Catholic; the schools run by the governments were secular and colonial.[21]

A very small number of Catholic secondary schools, mainly to provide for the equally small section of middle-class Catholics, was established alongside Protestant secondary schools. It was not until the end of the nineteenth and the beginning of the twentieth century that legislation was passed providing for public sector provision of secondary education, in what were termed 'high schools'. These high schools provided the base for the secondary school systems which developed in each of the states after Federation in 1901. Catholic schools, both primary and secondary, now had to struggle on for over sixty years without any state assistance. They were able to do so only because of their large unpaid teaching force of nuns, brothers and priests.

Much of the Church's effort in education in Australia by the end of the nineteenth century and the beginning of the twentieth century was part of its wider scheme of breaking down the link between being Catholic and being working class. In this way, it sought to overcome the Protestant ascendancy's practices aimed at keeping Catholics in a subordinate position. Australia was primarily British and Protestant, but there was a fear that there were 'enemies within the walls'. The dominant view was that the Catholic minority was composed of political agitators intent on spreading revolutionary ideas. The 'sacred fortress' and 'church militant' mentality now being preached by Rome also fuelled Protestant fears that Catholics might be entertaining a Papist overthrow of the state.

Protestant fears lingered on into the first half of the twentieth century. Sectarianism was widespread, with many businesses adopting a 'no Catholic need apply' position. The Church responded with a policy aimed at elevating the status of Catholics in Australian society so that the status of the Church itself would, in turn, be elevated. Education was a major plank in this policy, eventually contributing to the development of a mind-set which gave Catholics a sense of purpose and a sense of identity of which they could be proud. Steadily, they moved up the social ladder. The situation, as recorded in the 1933 census has been summarized as follows:

> [B]readwinners describing themselves as Catholic, both male and female, were more likely to be unemployed than those of other denominations, and about two-thirds of nominally Catholic breadwinners had an annual income £40 or more below the Australian average. At the same time, one-fifth of the Catholic breadwinners were in the top two income categories, earning over £207 per year. This proportion was less than that of the population as a whole, but only by three per cent.[22]

The 1947 census showed further progress. Even though Catholics were still under-represented in business and higher education, they had moved solidly into the public service and the professions, and were no longer characteristically poorer than other denominations".[23]

Notwithstanding their social progress, however, Australian Catholics' sense of suspicion, bitterness and resentment lived on throughout the first half of the twentieth century. This was reinforced by the feeling of injustice at being deprived of financial assistance for their schools and the continuing sectarianism they experienced in the workplace. Thus, throughout the period 1922–65, Catholics in Australia continued to see themselves "as 'other' than the mainstream".[24] The Catholic school was a major instrument in preserving the sense of 'otherness'. This time, however, unlike in previous decades, it did so by supporting a new confidence amongst 'the faithful'. Australian Catholics no longer persevered with a ghetto mentality. Rather, they were concerned with maintaining their improved social position and with moving more assertively into the wider society, viewing the world "not so much as a trap to be avoided as an environment in need of good influence".[25]

The well-spring of the 'good influences' which Catholics sought to disseminate throughout Australian society was the worldview composed of the four characteristic features of the process of Catholic education considered throughout this book: it was conducted within an authoritarian framework, a major emphasis was placed on religious instruction and on ensuring that schooling had a religious atmosphere which was all-pervasive, particular gender roles were promoted on the grounds that they constituted those roles best fitted to ensuring the salvation of 'the faithful', and there was a very strong Irish influence in pupils' experience of schooling. The worldview of which these features were component parts was, of course, also shaped by the Catholic home, by attendance at Sunday Mass, and by the many spiritual and recreational organizations run by the Church. Also, it was a view which came under very little pressure during the period 1922–65. It is true that there was some dilution of the authoritarian atmosphere in certain schools as teachers who were members of religious orders had their perspectives broadened by availing themselves much more of university education. Accompanying this development was a move towards less dogmatic approaches to the teaching of religion. Yet, within the overall context, these changes only had a very slight influence. This was no more than was to be expected given Rome's degree of supervision of religious orders and its regular statements reinforcing the view that the approach taken on the place of religion in Catholic schools was the correct one. Equally, the gender roles emphasized for the majority of the Catholic population, while justified on religious grounds, largely matched Australian stereotypes.

The direct Irish influence in pupils' experience of schooling and the impregnation of the other three distinctive features of the process of education in Catholic schools in Australia with Irish Catholicism were also maintained. It was only in the 1930s that the Irish monopoly of the Australian hierarchy was broken with the appointment of a significant number of Australian-born bishops.[26] Australian-born priests did not come to outnumber those who were Irish-born until the same decade, and even then they knew only one model of Catholicism, that of the Irish Catholic Church. Also, it is not as if the influence of first-generation Irish clerics disappeared; from the 1930s to the 1960s Irish priests continued to arrive in Australia in significant numbers,[27] while the female religious teaching orders continued to recruit girls from Ireland to become nuns and teach in their schools.

The Australian experience, as considered in this book, serves as one example to illustrate that the salient features of Catholicism and Catholic education were modified in different countries by the particular circumstances in operation. A consideration of the situation in Britain also helps in this regard. Here, from 1833, government grants were provided as a contribution to the cost of building schools incurred by various voluntary societies.[28] While originally Catholic schools were excluded from this scheme, the demand for places became urgent after the Great Famine which commenced in Ireland in 1845 produced a massive influx of immigrants, particularly in the cities of Liverpool and Manchester. Soon Catholic education was being encouraged by the British state with the extension of government grant aid to the Church's schools through the Catholic Poor School Committee, established in 1847.

Unlike the situation in Australia, government financial assistance in various forms continued for Catholic education in Britain up to the present day. Hickman[29] has argued that this was largely because successive British governments saw Catholic schools as serving their interests in pacifying a potentially rebellious minority by incorporating its members into British society. She also suggests a degree of collusion between the Catholic bishops and the British state over this arrangement. The Church's main interest was in retaining the Catholic allegiance of its new members, and it aimed to achieve this by strengthening their Catholic identity at the expense of their children's Irish identity. In other words, in return for financial support and autonomy over the Catholic schools, the Catholic bishops contributed to the suppression of the cultural identity of Irish pupils in Britain by stressing the Catholic, to the exclusion of the Irish, dimension in their lives. This connivance of the Catholic Church and the state in the 'incorporation' of Irish working-class children into the culture of the dominant Protestant community continued well into the middle of the twentieth century, when Catholics constituted over 10 per cent of the British population. Indeed, it has only been in the last fifteen to twenty years that Irish studies has been offered in British schools to pupils of Irish ancestry as part of a new policy of multiculturalism.

The situation in Ireland itself was different.[30] Here, by the second half of the nineteenth century, the Catholic Church had become a powerful interest group pressing its claims in educational matters with great tenacity. It had a commitment to the principle of denominational education at all levels. Its efforts ensured that the majority of 'national' schools, which had been intended to provide a multi-denominational primary school education, were attended by Catholic pupils only and managed by the Catholic clergy. Following independence from Britain in 1922, successive governments left the management of primary and secondary schools in the hands of the Church, while accepting financial responsibility for their maintenance.

Satisfied that its interests were safeguarded by the schools' administrative structures, the Church, in turn, supported the state's policy of reviving the Irish language by promoting it within the educational system.[31] The consensus was that the children of the nation should be taught Irish as part of their national heritage. Equally, the belief was that for the nation to survive it needed to demonstrate a separate cultural and political existence from Britain; a difference expressed through the Irish language. Since Irish was no longer the first language of the great majority it had to be revived, and the schools were the most obvious instrument. For many of the clergy, as well, the promotion of the Irish language was justified as it could lead to the development of a barrier against Anglicization and Protestant thought.

The situation in the United States was different yet again. Here, from the beginning of the nineteenth century, immigration had created an increasingly diverse Catholic population in terms of language, culture and ethnic loyalties. Furthermore, migrants found themselves within an institution whose governance was permeated by democracy at the local Church-community level. On this, Bryk, Lee and Holland have noted that "the roots of egalitarianism, ecumenism and democratization had been established by 1800"[32] in the American Catholic Church and that while these forces were largely submerged in terms of official actions by the institutional Church until the 1960s, "they remained alive in the work and thought of individual religious and lay members".[33]

To make the latter observation is not to overlook the opposition of the Church to the 'common school' idea. This idea was spawned by the perception around the beginning of the 1830s that the increase in Catholic immigrants was sufficient to pose a threat to the Anglo-Saxon Protestant majority. The argument emerged that only through educating all children together in a 'common school' regardless of religious or social background, "could America sustain a harmonious community amidst its diversity".[34] Many Catholics perceived this as an attempt to assimilate them into the majority tradition and there was much support for the bishops when, in 1884, they commanded Catholic parents to send their children to parochial schools. This development, as Bryk, Lee and Holland have pointed out, formalized the separate school system which had already been emerging. Yet, they also argued that, far from promoting separatism and establishing a divisive ethnic politics threatening to democracy, events developed quite differently:

> [M]ost immigrants did not want the total isolation of a ghetto Church. They sought a piece of the economic promise that was America, and therefore they wanted schools to teach the English language and some of the mores of American life.[35]

A strong sense of pluralism was also maintained amongst American Catholics through the establishment and maintenance of ethnic schools.

Australia, by contrast, perpetuated the notion of a monolithic Church on the Irish model. The Irish dominance of the clerical ranks was a smooth arrangement in the nineteenth century, as most of the early Catholics in Australia were Irish-born and thus were comfortable with their pastors. By the early 1900s, however, Catholics in Australia had become second-or-third generation Irish. Immigration during the period 1921–33 led to an increase in European Catholics in the country. This European influence expanded greatly after World War Two when large numbers of Polish, Italian and Yugoslavian Catholic migrants entered the country. While they brought distinct and diverse religious traditions with them, the reaction of the institutional Church was, as Massam puts it, "a policy of spiritual assimilation".[36] The same assimilationist policy applied when the new migrants attended Catholic schools.

Notwithstanding the examples presented so far, aimed at illustrating how Catholicism was modified in different countries by the particular circumstances in operation, it is also important to keep in mind that the salient features of Catholicism and Catholic education were universal and could be recognized everywhere. Up until the middle of the 1960s the Catholic Church, the largest Christian body in the world, saw itself as being engaged in battle against the forces of evil in this world to ensure that all would be united in the heavenly court. To this end, it operated with military-like precision due to the way its many institutions were organized:

> [T]here was a uniform governance of disparate structures, such as monasteries, universities, hospitals, as well as religious orders, exercised through the congregations of the Roman Curia...A huge 'army' of priests and the men and women of the various religious orders operated this vast enterprise known to the world at large as the Roman Catholic Church. At the head of the Church's corporate life there was the supreme pontiff, the vicar of Christ, the Pope.[37]

Catholic education under this regime had a strong, straightforward and often taken-for-granted aim, namely, to serve the development of faith. What this entailed was spelt out by Pope Pius XI, in 1929, in his encyclical *Divinii Illius Magistri: On the Christian Education of Youth*.[38] Here the view of the person adopted was a very cautious one, with "much talk of sin, weakness and a will flawed by desire".[39]

In its introduction, the encyclical considered education in general and gave particular attention to Catholic education. Kelty has summarized the position taken as follows:

> [T]he term 'education' follows a classical and traditional Catholic usage. Education refers essentially to moral formation as a result of which the person acts always in accord with one's ultimate purpose or teleology, i.e. in accord with the moral good...there is no final goal for humanity other than determined by God, revealed by Christ and taught by the Church, which has the right to claim possession of integral truth about human nature and its teleology. In this view of education, the pursuit of the moral good is to act according to Christian principles, because only Christianity has the supernatural principles pertaining to the ultimate state of humanity. Therefore, the only adequate and perfect education is Christian education.[40]

Kelty goes on to argue that such a deeply suspicious view of human nature led to some reactionary positions being adopted in the encyclical with regard to educational practice. In particular, 'pedagogic naturalism' was said to be pitted against the doctrines of original sin and grace, and therefore was held to be unsound. This position not only inhibited the embracing of experiential approaches to education, "but it supported also the memorable sections of the encyclical which condemned both sex instruction and coeducation".[41] Such a view remained in the ascendancy up until the beginning of the 1960s.

It seemed as if nothing short of a great shock would shift the authoritarian, hierarchical and dogmatic Catholic Church. The shock came, however, when Pope John XXIII announced the convening of a second Vatican Council. Between 1962 and 1965 the council brought together twenty-five hundred bishops from around the world to deliberate. The end result was "revolutionary, profoundly affecting every aspect of Catholic life".[42] Hornsby-Smith sums up as follows:

> The Vatican Council's emphasis on collegiality and participation by all the 'people of God' can be seen as indicating a shift within a changing world to an 'organic' management structure with far more emphasis on lateral consultation than vertical command...There was a movement away from the legalistic following of institutional rules and regulations to a concern with how Christians were to live fully human and liberated lives.[43]

Ironically, the new outlook led to a dramatic decline in the number of nuns, religious brothers and priests over the next fifteen years. This could have spelt the demise of Catholic education in Australia. Already, Catholic schools were on the verge of collapse owing to lack of finance. The conservative political parties—the Liberal Party and the Country Party—had, however, begun to relax their opposition to government assistance for church schools in the 1950s and 1960s. By 1969, virtually all of the states were giving recurrent aid to non-government schools in the form of equal per capita grants, under policies agreed to by the federal government.[44] Then, after the return of the Labor Party to government in 1972, the great majority of Catholic schools obtained approximately 80 per cent of their costs from Australian state or federal governments, and became able to apply for capital grants for refurbishing or extending schools.

Catholic education now underwent a transformation. Catholic education offices were established in all dioceses and these tended to be staffed by full-time professionals with administrative support personnel. Parents became much more involved in educational decision-making. There was a huge increase in lay-teacher presence in schools, while many of the nuns, religious brothers and priests who continued to work alongside them took up the new challenge to become more open to the world. The Catholic education sector, like the other education sectors in Australia, encouraged heuristic pedagogical approaches and offered revitalized school subjects to meet social needs. Also, there was a shift in the teaching of religion to 'experiential catechesis' which endeavored to lead each child to consider his or her own life and to discern religious meaning in it as a basis for comprehending the core doctrinal message of the Church.

To present a major exposition on the latter developments would necessitate opening up a whole new chapter and bring one well beyond the central focus of this book. What is noteworthy at this point, however, is that the process of education in Catholic schools in Australia was influenced greatly by the Second Vatican Council's work and by the position statements of the Congregation for Catholic Education which was established to develop this work. It is true that the overall aim of Catholic education has remained the spiritual growth and development of all Catholics through a process which includes preparation for a fuller life in eternity. The various interpretations on how this should translate into educational practices, however, place much more of an emphasis than in the past on having a deep respect for the individual, on the building of a Christian community, and on social justice issues.

Arguing within the Australian context, McLaughlin, in a recent comprehensive review of Church documents, challenges the traditional view of Catholic education within the nation. He concludes that the primary purpose of the Catholic school in this post-modern era is:

> To generate a challenging, authentic educational environment, faithful to the Catholic tradition of offering a synthesis of faith and culture, which, while promoting integral human growth, provides a catalyst for students to take the opportunity to initiate or continue a personal relationship with Christ, that witnesses its practical expression in an active, inclusive care for others, while confronting contemporary injustices in economic and social structures, all of which gives meaning to, and enriches human existence, and contributes to a fuller human life.[45]

To recognize the expression of such vibrant positions is not, of course, to contend that Catholic education is now without threat. Indeed, there are those who argue that the threat is greater than ever. They point out how in the past, just like in the United States, the value of education as a vehicle for social mobility very quickly became apparent to Australian Catholic educators and parents, but then go on to note that a high price is now being paid. On this, McLaughlin, for example, states that certain Catholic schools in Australia have adopted pecuniary values and successfully generated an upwardly mobile, Catholic middle class indistinguishable within secular Australian society. Equally, there have been recent exchanges in the United States on the 'eliting' of Catholic schools[46] which led to Baker and Riordan being pitted against Greely, "the dean of Catholic educational researchers".[47]

There are also those who consider that Catholic schools in Australia have been overly influenced by the contemporary education 'industry', which tends to see knowledge as utilitarian and students as products. This situation is compounded by the pride generated when it is pointed out that there are studies, particularly in the United States[48] and Britain,[49] which show a Catholic school effect on tests of academic achievement; studies which are seized upon by the 'new right' and promoters of government vouchers as demonstrating the failure of public schools. And then there are those who like to observe that many Catholic schools display some of the central characteristics of 'effective schools'. What they fail to appreciate, however, as Bryk, Lee and Holland point out, is that underlying such characteristics "is a rich set of experiences, ideas, and symbols, which together constitute a tradition that continues to shape [Catholic] school life today".[50] These experiences, ideas and symbols have been generated, molded and adapted over a long period of time and their influence is dependent, at least in part, on an appreciation of the historical circumstances which give them meaning. Thus, one would be naive in the extreme if one thought that all public schools had to do was graft onto themselves the characteristics of Catholic schools and they would then become equally successful.

In a similar vein, an appreciation of the history of Catholic education is important if one is to look to Catholic social theory to justify contemporary developments in the management and administration of educational systems. A consideration of some recent thinking in Australia serves to demonstrate this point. The background is the Church's emphasis on the 'person-in-community' notion. This notion asserts that the progress of the individual is integrally related to that of others. Consequently, both individual good and community good must be fostered. Therefore education, it is argued, has a major role to play in the Church's commitment to the dignity of persons and the building of community. The argument which follows is that Catholic schools should be managed and administered according to three principles. The first is the principle of subsidiarity. This requires that in designing any system one should start at the local level and only pass on to higher levels what cannot be performed by the local body. The second principle, pluriformity, emphasizes the importance of encouraging diversity. The third principle, that of complementarity, means that "each part of the enterprise will dovetail, will complement, help and encourage the other parts, and will not impede them".[51]

It is interesting that scholars like Beare have drawn attention to these principles and are admiring of the potential which they hold for restructuring the state educational systems in Australia. A number of cautionary notes, however, need to be sounded. First, while the pattern of provision of Catholic education in Australia up until the early 1970s might appear to have been shaped by the principles of Catholic social teaching noted above, with many schools operating largely independent of each other, the influencing factors were that these schools were established where a need was considered to exist rather than as part of a well-planned system of education and, more often than not, were managed by religious orders which were independent of each other and which jealously guarded this independence. Secondly, there is a need to understand the theoretical foundations of Catholic social teaching. These have already been outlined in some detail in Chapter 4 of this book. What needs to be pointed out at this stage, however, is that if contemporary educational theorists are to draw attention to the associated principles of subsidiarity, pluriformity and complementarity in justifying notions such as that of a devolved educational system, then it must be stressed that these principles do not emanate from an industrial psychology model which would see devolution as being important because of the possibilities it might hold out for greater efficiency and productivity. Rather, they are principles which developed out of a commitment to the importance of maintaining and promoting the dignity of the human person at a time when many were caught between the anarchy of traditional capitalism and the totalitarianisms of right and left.

It is also instructive to note that Catholic education in England and Wales is currently largely following the 'managerial' trend being promoted by the state. On this, Sullivan has sounded the following warning:

> [T]oo great a readiness to map out performance indicators, programmes of study attainment targets, developments plans, and the scaffolding of competencies required at various stages throughout the teaching profession can lead to specifications which are too elaborate, leave too little to chance, reduce the possibility of appropriate reciprocity and interaction between teachers and learners and slip too easily into conceiving education as a technique requiring merely one-way transmission.[52]

He goes on to point out that the British state's encouragement of increased competition between schools, which was intended to act as a lever for raising standards and widening choice, has been seen by some Catholics as having effects which are detrimental to sound education, damaging to pastoral care and undermining community spirit; ideals which are central to the 'new' thrust of Catholic education. Similarly, Bezzina,[53] referring to current trends on the Australian educational scene, has argued that the uncritical adoption of the mechanisms of competition and control has the capacity to produce outcomes which run counter to some of the core values of Catholic education, particularly with respect to the nature and purposes of Catholic schools, and the principles of social justice.

In Australia, then, as in much of the English-speaking world, the Catholic Church has some major decisions to make regarding its future involvement in education. It can, on the one hand, depart radically from the traditions outlined in this book, become involved in packaging education as a commodity and head down a road which will result in its schools being assimilated into the general Australian culture to the point of being indistinguishable from it. On the other hand, it can take steps to maintain the pattern of being a complement to public schools, while promoting curricular and pedagogical practices in tune with more recent Catholic thinking on the pursuit of the common good in the education of young people. To take the latter step would be to build on those developments since the 1960s which moved the process of education in Catholic schools in Australia well beyond those features which made it distinctive during the period 1922–65, and thus open up a whole new chapter in the history of education in the nation.

Notes

[1] E. J. King, *Other Schools and Ours—Comparative Education for Today* (London: Holt, Rinehart and Winston, 1973), p. 127.

[2] M. P. Magray, *The Transforming Power of the Nuns: Women, Religion and Cultural Change in Ireland, 1750–1900* (New York: Oxford University Press, 1998), p. 4.

[3] Ibid., pp. 32-49.

[4] Ibid., p. 42.

[5] Ibid., p. 6.

[6] T. Inglis, *Moral Monopoly: The Rise and Fall of the Catholic Church in Modern Ireland* (Dublin: University College Dublin Press, 1998), p. 134.

[7] S. J. Connolly, *Priests and People in Pre-Famine Ireland 1780–1845* (Dublin: Gill and Macmillan, 1982), p. 47.

[8] T. Inglis, *Moral Monopoly: The Rise and Fall of the Catholic Church in Modern Ireland*, p. 135.

[9] Ibid., p. 136.

[10] J. J. Lee, 'Continuity and change in Ireland, 1945-70', in J. J. Lee (ed.), *Ireland 1945–70* (Dublin: Gill and Macmillan, 1979), p. 166.

[11] See T. Fahey, 'Catholicism and industrial society in Ireland', in J. H. Goldthorpe and C. T. Whelan (eds.), *The Development of Industrial Society in Ireland* (Oxford: Oxford University Press, 1994), p. 167.

[12] J. J. Lee, 'Continuity and change in Ireland, 1945-70', p. 167.

[13] S. Connolly, *Religion and Society in Nineteenth Century Ireland* (Dundalk, Ireland: Dundalgan Press, 1985), p. 55.

[14] S. Connolly, *Religion and Society in Nineteenth Century Ireland*, p. 12.

[15] Ibid., p. 27.

[16] Ibid., p. 54.

[17] J. J. Ó'Ríordáin, *Irish Catholics: Tradition and Transition* (Dublin: Veritas Publications, 1980), p. 74.

[18] D. H. Akenson, *The Irish Diaspora—A Primer*, p. 104.

[19] Ibid.

[20] Ibid.

[21] D. White, *Education and the State: Federal Involvement in Educational Policy Development*, p. 10.

[22] K. Massam, *Sacred Threads: Catholic Spirituality in Australia 1922–1962* (Sydney: University of New South Wales Press, 1996), p. 18.

[23] Ibid.

[24] K. Massam, *Sacred Thread: Catholic Spirituality in Australia 1922–1962*, p. 33.

[25] Ibid., p. 31.

[26] Ibid.

[27] Ibid.

[28] The following account is based on that in M. J. Hickman, 'Catholicism and the nation state in nineteenth century Britain', in M. Eaton, J. Longmore and A. Naylor (eds.), *Commitment to Diversity: Catholics and Education in a Changing World* (London and New York: Cassell, 2000), pp. 47–66.

[29] Ibid.

[30] I have dealt with this in detail in T. A. O'Donoghue, *The Catholic Church and the Secondary School Curriculum in Ireland, 1922–1962* (New York: Peter Lang, 1999).

[31] Ibid.

[32] A. S. Bryk, V. E. Lee and P. B. Holland, *Catholic Schools and the Common Good*, p. 23.

[33] Ibid.

[34] Ibid., p. 24.

[35] Ibid., p. 27.

[36] K. Massam, *Sacred Threads: Catholic Spirituality in Australia 1922–1962*, p. 22.

[37] B. Kelty, 'Catholic education: The historical context', in D. McLaughlin (ed.), *The Catholic School: Paradoxes and Challenges* (Strathfield, NSW, Australia: St. Paul's Publications, 2000), p. 13.

[38] Pius XI, *Divinii Illius Magistri: On the Christian Education of Youth* (London: Catholic Truth Society, 1929).

[39] B. Kelty, 'Catholic education: The historical context', p. 27.

[40] Ibid., p. 21.

[41] Ibid., p. 27.

[42] A. S. Bryk, V. E. Lee and P. B. Holland, *Catholic Schools and the Common Good*, p. 46.

[43] M. P. Hornsby-Smith, 'Social and religious transformations in Ireland: A case of secularisation', in J. H. Goldthorpe and C. T. Whelan (eds.), *The Development of Industrial Society in Ireland*, p. 271.

[44] A. O'Brien, *Blazing a Trail: Catholic Education in Victoria 1963-1980* (Melbourne: David Lovell Publishing, 1999), p. 29.

[45] D. McLaughlin, 'Quo vadis Catholic education?' in D. McLaughlin (ed.), *The Catholic School: Paradoxes and Challenges*, p. 111.

[46] See D. P. Baker and C. Riordan, 'The eliting of the common American Catholic school and the national education crisis', *Phi Delta Kappan*, September 1988, pp. 16–23; and A. Greeley, 'The so-called failure of Catholic schools', *Phi Delta Kappan*, September 1988, pp. 24–25.

[47] J. Youniss and J. A. McLellan, 'Catholic schools in perspective: Religious identity, achievement, and citizenship', *Phi Delta Kappan*, October 1999, p. 105.

[48] Ibid., pp. 108–109.

[49] See, for example, A. B. Morris, 'The academic performance of Catholic schools', *School Organisation*, Vol. 14, No. 1, 1994, pp. 81–89.

[50] A. S. Bryk, V. E. Lee and P. B. Holland, *Catholic Schools and the Common Good*, p. 16.

[51] H. Beare, *What is the Next Quantum Leap for School Systems in Australia? The 1994 Currie Lecture* (Melbourne: Australian Council for Educational Administration, 1995), p. 8.

[52] J. Sullivan, 'Wrestling with managerialism', in M. Eaton, J. Longmore and A. Naylor (eds.), *Commitment to Diversity: Catholics and Education in a Changing World*, p. 242.

[53] M. Bezzina, 'To market, to market?', *Catholic School Studies*, Vol. 73, No. 2, 2000, pp. 4–11.

References

Akenson, D. H. *The Irish Diaspora—A Primer*. Toronto: P. D. Meaney Company, Inc., 1996.

Altenbaugh, R. J. 'Oral history, American teachers and the social history of schooling'. In R. J. Altenbaugh (ed.), *The Teacher's Voice*. London: Falmer Press, 1992, pp. 1–6.

———. 'Oral history, American teachers and the social history of schooling'. *Cambridge Journal of Education*. Vol. 27, No. 3, 1997, pp. 313–330.

Angus, L. 'Class, culture and curriculum: A study of continuity and change in a Catholic school'. In R. Bates, L. Smith, L. Angus and P. Watkins (eds.), *Continuity and Change in Catholic Education: An Ethnography of Christian Brothers College*. Victoria, Australia: Deakin University, 1982, pp. 26–63.

Arnold, J. *Mother Superior Woman Inferior*. Blackburn, Victoria, Australia: Dove Communications, 1985.

Austin, A. G. *The Australian Government School 1830–1914: Select Documents With Commentary*. Carlton, Victoria, Australia: Pitman Publishing Pty. Ltd., 1975.

Australian Schools Commission (Report of the Interim Committee for the Australian Schools Commission, P. Karmel, Chairman). *Schools in Australia*. Canberra, Australia: Australian Government Printing Service, 1973.

Baker, D. P. and Riordan, C. 'The eliting of the common American Catholic school and the national education crisis'. *Phi Delta Kappan*. September 1988, pp. 16–23.

Barcan, A. *A Short History of Education in New South Wales*. Sydney: Martindale Press, 1965.

Barcan, A. *Two Centuries of Education in New South Wales*. Kensington, New South Wales, Australia: New South Wales University Press, 1988.

Beare, H. *What is the Next Quantum Leap for School Systems in Australia? The 1994 Currie Lecture*. Melbourne: Australian Council for Educational Administration, 1995.

Bennett, R. W. 'Changes in the Catholic school system in the Maitland Diocese resulting from an increased proportion of lay teachers staffing these schools', unpublished M.Ed. thesis, University of Newcastle, 1978.

Bernstein, M. B. *Nuns*. Glasgow: Collins, 1978.

Bezzina, M. 'To market, to market?' *Catholic School Studies*, Vol. 73, No. 2, 2000, pp. 4–11.

Bollen, J. D., Cahill, A. E., Mansfield, B. and O' Farrell, P. 'Australian religious history 1960–80'. *Journal of Religious History*. Vol. 11, 1980, pp. 8–44.

Bourke, J. E. 'Roman Catholic schools'. In D. A. Jecks (ed.), *Influences in Australian Education*. Perth, Australia: Carroll's, 1974, pp. 245–266.

Brice, I. D. 'Australian boys' schools and the historical constructions of masculinity'. Proceedings of the ANZHES Annual Conference, Sydney, Australia, 1995.

———. 'Ethnic masculinities in Australian boys' schools—Scots and Irish secondary schools in late nineteenth century Australia'. Proceedings of the ISCHE Annual Conference, Sydney, 1998.

Brigidine Sisters, The. *Directory of the Brigidine Sisters*. New South Wales: The Brigidine Sisters, 1955.

Bruner, J. *The Process of Education*. New York: Vantage, 1960.

Bryk, A. S., Lee, V. E. and Holland, P. B. *Catholic Schools and the Common Good*. Cambridge: Harvard University Press, 1993.

Burford, K. E. *Unfurrowed Fields. A Josephite Story NSW 1872–1972*. Sydney: St. Joseph's Convent, 1991.

Burley, S. 'Lost leaders from the convent and the classroom 1880–1925'. In J. McMahon, H. Neidhart and J. Chapman (eds.), *Leading the Catholic School*. Richmond, Victoria, Australia: Spectrum, 1997, pp. 49–62.

———. 'Resurrecting the religious experience of Catholic girls' schooling in South Australia in the 1920s'. Proceedings of the ANZHES Annual Conference, Auckland, New Zealand, 1998.

Campion, E. 'Irish religion in Australia'. *The Australasian Catholic Record*. Vol. 55, 1978, pp. 10–14.

Christian Brothers, The. *Directory and Rules of the Congregation of the Brothers of the Christian Schools of Ireland*. Dublin: The Christian Brothers, 1927.

Christie, D. and Smith, P. 'Teachers' careers in Catholic schools'. In R. MacClean and P. McKenzie (eds.), *Australian Teachers' Careers*. Hawthorn, Victoria, Australia: Australian Council for Educational Research, 1991, pp. 211–240.

Clancy, L. *The Collapsible Man*. Melbourne: Outback Press, 1975.

Clarke, E. *Female Teachers in Queensland State Schools: A History 1860–1983*. Brisbane: Department of Education Policy and Information Services Branch, June 1985.

Coldrey, B. M. 'The influence of Irish traditions on the policies and professional training of the Christian Brothers in Victoria, 1868–1930', unpublished M.Ed. thesis, The University of Melbourne, 1973.

———. *Child Migration and the Western Australian Boys' Homes*. Victoria, Australia: Tamanaraik Publishing, 1991.

———. 'A most unenviable reputation: the Christian Brothers and school discipline over two centuries'. *History of Education*. Vol. 21, No. 3, 1992, pp. 277–289.

Concilium Legionis Mariae. *The Official Handbook of the Legion of Mary*. Dublin: The Legion of Mary, 1969.

Congregations of Religious Women in Western Australia. *In Search of the Promise of Something Special: Life with a Purpose*. Perth,

Australia: Congregations of Religious Women in Western Australia, nd.

Connell, R. W. *Masculinities*. London: Polity Press, 1995.

Connell, W. F. *Reshaping Australian Education: 1960–1985*. Hawthorn, Victoria, Australia: Australian Council for Educational Research, 1993.

Connolly, S. J. *Priests and People in Pre-Famine Ireland 1780–1845*. Dublin: Gill and Macmillan, 1982.

––––––. *Religion and Society in Nineteenth Century Ireland*. Dundalk, Ireland: Dundalgan Press, 1985.

Cooper, A. 'A select bibliography'. *The Australasian Catholic Record*. Vol. 25, No. 2, 1998, pp. 164–179.

Corrigan, U. 'The achievements of the Catholic people of Australia in the field of education'. In Australian Catholic Education Congress. *Australian Catholic Education Congress: Adelaide, Australia, 1936*. Melbourne: The Advocate Press, 1936, pp. 292–294.

Cuban, L. *How Teachers Taught: Constancy and Change in American Classrooms, 1890–1980*. New York: Longman, 1984.

Dams, K., Depaepe, M. and Simon, F. 'Sneaking into school: Classroom history at work'. In I. Grosvenor, M. Lawn and K. Rousmaniere (eds.), *Silences and Images*. New York: Peter Lang Publishing, 1999, pp. 13–46.

Dening, G. and Kennedy, D. *Xavier Portraits*. Melbourne: Old Xavierians' Association, 1993.

Duffy, P. J. *The Lay Teacher*. Dublin: Fallons, 1967.

Duncan, B. J. 'An analysis of the primary teacher education of the Sisters of Mercy, the Christian Brothers and their lay teachers in Queensland from 1859 to 1979', unpublished Ph.D. thesis, The University of Queensland, 1984.

Eaton, M., Longmore, J. and Naylor, A. (eds.), *Commitment to Diversity: Catholics and Education in a Changing World*. London and New York: Cassell, 2000.

Edgar, D. *Introduction to Australian Society: A Sociological Perspective.* Sydney: Prentice-Hall, 1980.

Episcopal Committee for Catholic Action, Social Justice Statement. *Christian Education in a Democratic Community.* Carnegie, Victoria, Australia: Renown, 1949.

Eraut, M., Goad, L. and Smith, G. *The Analysis of Curriculum Materials.* Brighton, England: University of Sussex, 1975.

Fahey, T. 'Catholicism and industrial society in Ireland'. In J. H. Goldthorpe and C. T. Whelan (eds.), *The Development of Industrial Society in Ireland.* Oxford: Oxford University Press, 1994, pp. 241–263.

Finkelstein, B. 'Classroom management in the United States'. In N. K. Shimahara (ed.), *Politics of Classroom Life: Classroom Life in International Perspective.* New York: Garland Publishing, Inc., 1998, pp. 11–48.

Finkelstein, B. *Governing the Young: Teacher Behaviour in Popular Primary Schools in Nineteenth Century United States.* London: Falmer Press, 1989.

Flannery, A. (ed.), *Vatican Council 11. The Conciliar and Post Conciliar Documents.* Dublin: Dominican Publications, 1975.

Flynn, M. *The Culture of Catholic Schools.* Homebush, NSW, Australia: St. Paul's Publications, 1993.

Fogarty, R. *Catholic Education in Australia 1806–1950.* Melbourne: Melbourne University Press, 1959.

Ford, O. 'Voices from below: Family, school and community in the Braybrook Plains 1854–1892', unpublished M.Ed. thesis, The University of Melbourne, 1993.

Franklin, B. *Building the American Community: The School Curriculum and the Search for Social Control.* Philadelphia: Falmer Press, 1986.

Gall, M. D. *Handbook for Evaluating and Selecting Curriculum Materials.* Boston: Allyn and Unwin, 1981.

Gardner, P. and Cunningham, P. 'Oral history and teachers' professional practice'. *Cambridge Journal of Education.* Vol. 27, No. 3, 1997, pp. 331–342.

Goodson, I. F. *School Subjects and Curriculum Change: The School Curriculum and the Search for Social Control.* Dover, New Hampshire: Croom Helm, 1983.

———. *Social Histories of the Secondary School Curriculum: Subjects for Study.* Dover, New Hampshire: Croom Helm, 1985.

———. *International Perspectives in Curriculum History.* Dover, New Hampshire: Croom Helm, 1987.

———. *The Making of Curriculum: Collected Essays.* New York: Falmer Press, 1988.

———. 'Studying school subjects', *Curriculum Perspectives.* Vol. 12, No. 1, 1992, pp. 23–26.

Goodson, I. V. and Hargreaves, A. (eds.), *Teachers' Professional Lives.* London: Falmer Press, 1996.

Greeley, A. 'The so-called failure of Catholic schools'. *Phi Delta Kappan.* September 1988, pp. 24–25.

Greening, W. A. 'The adaptation of the Irish Christian Brothers' education system to Australian conditions in the nineteenth century', unpublished Ph.D. thesis, The University of Melbourne, 1989.

Hamilton, J. 'Faith and Football: Masculinities at Christian Brothers' College, Wakefield Street, 1879–1912, unpublished M.Ed. thesis, The University of Adelaide, 2000.

Hanrahan, M. B. 'A definite syllabus of religious instruction with regional variations'. In Australian Catholic Education Congress, *Australian Catholic Education Congress, Adelaide, Australia.* Melbourne: The Advocate Press, 1937, pp. 101–110.

Hatch, J. A. and Wisniewski, R. *Life History and Narrative.* London: Falmer Press, 1995.

Hawke, V. 'Treaties and bargains with God'. In K. Nelson and D. Nelson (eds.), *Sweet Mothers, Sweet Maids.* Ringwood, Victoria, Australia: Penguin Books, 1986, pp. 1–12.

Henderson, A. *Mary MacKillop's Sisters: A Life Unveiled.* Sydney: Harper-Collins, 1997.

Hickman, M. J. 'Catholicism and the nation state in nineteenth century Britain'. In M. Eaton, J. Longmore and A. Naylor (eds.), *Commitment to Diversity: Catholics and Education in a Changing World.* London and New York: Cassell, 2000, pp. 47–66.

Hogan, S. M. 'A crusade for vocations to the teaching orders'. In Australian Catholic Education Congress. *Australian Catholic Education Congress Adelaide Australia.* Melbourne: The Advocate Press, 1937, pp. 137–155.

Hornsby–Smith, M. P. 'Social and religious transformations in Ireland: A case of secularisation'. In J. H. Goldthorpe and C. T Whelan (eds.), *The Development of Industrial Society in Ireland.* Oxford: Oxford University Press, 1994, pp. 265–290.

Huberman, M. *The Lives of Teachers.* London: Falmer Press, 1993.

Inglis, T. *Moral Monopoly: The Rise and Fall of the Catholic Church in Modern Ireland.* Dublin: University College Dublin Press, 1998.

Institute of the Blessed Virgin Mary, The. *Rules IBVM.* Dublin: IBVM, 1914.

Irish Catholic Directory and Almanac. Dublin: James Duffy and Co. Ltd., 1940.

Kelty. B. 'Catholic education: The historical context'. In D. McLaughlin (ed.), *The Catholic School: Paradoxes and Challenges.* Strathfield, NSW, Australia: St. Paul's Publications, 2000, pp. 9–30.

Kennedy, S. *Faith and Feminism: Catholic Women's Struggle for Self-Expression.* Sydney: Studies in the Christian Movement, 1985.

King, A. R. and Brownell, J. A. *The Curriculum and the Disciplines of Knowledge.* New York: John Wiley and Sons, 1966.

King, E. J. *Other Schools and Ours—Comparative Education for Today.* London: Holt, Rinehart and Winston, 1973.

Kliebard, H. M. *The Struggle for the American Curriculum, 1893–1958.* Boston: Routledge and Kegan Paul, 1986.

Koch, K. *The Doubleman.* London: Angus and Robertson, 1955.

Kotre, J. *Outliving the Self: Generativity and the Interpretation of Lives.* Baltimore: Johns Hopkins University Press, 1984.

Kyle, N. K. *Her Natural Destiny.* NSW, Australia: New South Wales University Press, 1986.

Kyle, N. K. (ed.). *Women as Educators in 19th and 20th Century Australia.* Wollongong, Australia: University of Wollongong, School of Learning Studies, 1989.

Lancy, D. F. *Qualitative Research in Education.* New York: Longman, 1993.

Lawlor, K. J. *Bishop Bernard D. Stewart and Resistance to the Reform of Religious Education in the Diocese of Sandhurst, 1950–1979,* unpublished Ph.D. thesis. La Trobe University, 1999.

Leavey, M. C. 'The relevance of St. Thomas Aquinas for Australian education'. In E. L. French (ed.), *Melbourne Studies in Education.* Melbourne: Melbourne University Press, 1964.

———. 'Religious education, school climate and achievement: A study of nine Catholic sixth-form girls' schools', unpublished Ph.D. thesis, Australian National University, 1972.

Lee, J. J. 'Continuity and change in Ireland, 1945–70'. In J. J. Lee (ed.), *Ireland 1945–70* Dublin: Gill and Macmillan, 1979, pp 166–177.

Lesko, N. *Symbolizing Society: Stories, Rites and Structure in a Catholic High School.* London: Falmer Press, 1988.

Lewis, C. N. 'Provision for the education of Catholic women in Australia since 1840', unpublished Ph.D. thesis, The University of Melbourne, 1990.

Mackinnon, A. 'A new point of departure'. *History of Education Review.* Vol. 13, No. 2, 1984, pp. 1–4.

Maclaine, A. G. *Australian Education: Progress, Problems and Prospects.* Sydney: Ian Novak, 1973.

Marsh, C. 'The development of a senior school geography curriculum in Western Australia 1964–1984'. In I. F. Goodson (ed.), *School Subjects and Curriculum Change: Case Studies in the Social History of Curriculum.* Dover, New Hampshire: Croom Helm, 1987, pp. 179–208.

McCulloch, G. *The Secondary Technical School: A Usable Past?* London: Falmer Press, 1990.

McCulloch, G., Jenkins, E. and Layton, D. *Technological Revolution. The Politics of School Science and Technology in England and Wales Since 1945.* London: Falmer Press, 1985.

McGrath, M. S. *These Women? Women Religious in the History of Australia. The Sisters of Mercy at Parramatta 1888–1988.* Sydney: The Sisters of Mercy, 1991.

McKenzie, M. M. 'Catholic religious women educators as agents of social change', unpublished M.A. thesis, Monash University, 1994.

McLaren, P. 'Making Catholics: The ritual production of conformity in a Catholic junior high school'. *Journal of Education.* Vol. 168, No. 2, 1986, pp. 55–77.

McLay, A. *Women Out of Their Sphere.* Perth, WA, Australia: Vanguard Press, 1992.

McLaughlin, D. 'Quo vadis Catholic education?' In D. McLaughlin (ed.), *The Catholic School: Paradoxes and Challenges.* Strathfield, New South Wales: St. Paul's Publications, 2000, pp. 31–120.

McMahon, J. T. 'A liturgical programme for schools'. *Australasian Catholic Record.* Vol. 8, No. 4, 1931, pp. 297–304.

MacGinley, M. R. *A Dynamic of Hope: Institutes of Women Religious in Australia.* Sydney: Crossing Press, 1996.

Magray, M. P. *The Transforming Power of the Nuns: Women, Religion and Cultural Change in Ireland, 1750–1900.* New York: Oxford University Press, 1998.

Massam, K. *Sacred Threads: Catholic Spirituality in Australia 1922–1962.* Sydney: University of New South Wales Press, 1996.

Measor, L. 'Interviewing: A strategy in qualitative research'. In G. R. Burgess (ed.), *Strategies of Educational Research.* London: Falmer Press, 1985, pp. 63–73.

Molony, J. *The Roman Mould of the Australian Catholic Church.* Melbourne: Melbourne University Press, 1969.

Morris, A. B. 'The academic performance of Catholic schools'. *School Organisation.* Vol. 14, No. 1, 1994, pp. 81–89.

Mossenson, D. *State Education in Western Australia, 1829–1960.* Perth, Western Australia: University of Western Australia Press, 1972.

Murphy, D. *A History of Irish Emigrant and Missionary Education.* Dublin: Four Courts Press, 2000.

Musgrave, P. W. *Society and the Curriculum in Australia.* Sydney: George Allen and Unwin, 1979.

———. 'To be an Australian? Secular and Catholic versions of national identity in primary school textbooks, 1895–1964'. Unpublished paper, School of Graduate Studies, Monash University, 1993.

Nelson, K and Nelson, D. (eds.), *Sweet Mothers, Sweet Maids.* Ringwood, Victoria, Australia: Penguin Books, 1986.

Oakley, B. 'Years of sawdust: the crack of the whip'. *The Secondary Teacher,* February 1967, p. 13.

O'Brien, A. *Blazing a Trail: Catholic Education in Victoria, 1963–1980.* Melbourne: David Lovell Publishing, 1999.

O'Donoghue, T. A. 'The Sacred Heart Mission and education in Papua 1885–1942'. *Journal of Educational Administration and History.* Vol. 25, No. 1, 1993, pp. 58–71.

———.*The Catholic Church and the Secondary School Curriculum in Ireland, 1922-1962.* New York: Peter Lang Publishing, 1999.

O'Dowd, L. 'Church, state and women: The aftermath of partition'. in C. Curtin, P. Jackson and B. O'Connor (eds.), *Gender in Irish Society.* Galway, Ireland: Officina Typographica, 1987, pp. 3–36.

O'Farrell, P. J. (ed.), *Documents in Australian Catholic History, Vol 1.* London: Geoffrey Chapman, 1969.

———. *The Catholic Church in Australia. A Short History: 1788-1967.* London: Geoffrey Chapman, 1969.

———. *The Irish in Australia.* Kensington, NSW, Australia: New South Wales University Press, 1993.

O'Grady, D. *Deschooling Kevin Carew.* Melbourne: Wren, 1974.

Ó'Ríordáin, J. J. *Irish Catholics: Tradition and Transition.* Dublin: Veritas Publications, 1980.

Orme, A. R. *The World's Landscapes.* London: Longman, 1970.

Piper, K. *Evaluation and the Social Sciences.* Canberra, Australia: Australian Government Printing Service, 1976.

Pius XI. *Divinii Illius Magistri: On the Christian Education of Youth.* London: Catholic Truth Society, 1929.

Plummer, K. *Documents of Life.* Sydney: Allen and Unwin, 1983.

Potts, A. 'Public and private schooling in Australia: Some historical and contemporary considerations'. *Phi Delta Kappan.* November 1999, pp. 242–245.

Praetz, H. *Building a School System: A Sociological Study of Catholic Education.* Melbourne: Melbourne University Press, 1980.

Presentation Sisters, The. *Constitutions of the Presentation Sisters.* Cork: Hickey and Byrne, 1928.

Price, M. H. *The Development of the Secondary School Curriculum.* Dover, New Hampshire: Croom Helm, 1986.

Prus, R. Symbolic Interaction and Ethnographic Research: Intersubjectivity and the Study of Human Lived Experience. Albany: State University of New York Press, 1996.

Ritzer, G. *Sociological Theory.* New York: Alfred A. Knopf, 1994.

St. Brigid's College. *St Brigid's College Callan Golden Jubilee Book 1999.* Callan, Ireland: St. Brigid's College, 1999.

Scott, M. 'Masculinities and national identity in Adelaide boys' secondary schools, 1880–1911'. Proceedings of the ANZHES Annual Conference, Auckland, New Zealand, 1998.

Selleck, R. J. W. and Sullivan, M. G. (eds.), *Not So Eminent Victorians.* Melbourne: Melbourne University Press, 1982.

Silver, H. 'Historiography of education'. In T. Husen and T. N. Postlethwaite (eds.), *The International Encyclopaedia of Education.* London: Pergamon, 1994, pp. 2607-2618.

Silver, H. 'Knowing and not knowing in the history of education'. *History of Education*, Vol. 21, No. 1, 1992, pp. 97–108.

Silver, H. 'Nothing but the present, or nothing but the past'. In P. Gordon (ed.), *The Study of Education: A Collection of Inaugural Lectures.* London: The Woburn Press, 1980.

Simons, H. *Conversation Piece.* London: Grant McIntyre, 1982.

Simpson, T. A. 'A historical review of microteaching', unpublished M.A. thesis, Macquarie University, 1987.

Sisters of Mercy, The. *Someone Just Like You* (np; nd) (recruitment pamphlet).

Sisters of Mercy, The. *A Guide for the Religious Called Sisters of Mercy.* London: Robson and Son. 1866.

———. *Constitutions of the Congregation of the Australian Union of the Sisters of Our Lady of Mercy.* Canberra, Australia: The Sisters of Mercy—General Motherhouse, 1960.

Sisters of Our Lady of the Missions, The. *You Did Not Chose Me: No. I Chose You.* Perth, WA, Australia: Sisters of Our Lady of the Missions, nd.

Sisters of Saint Joseph of the Most Sacred Heart of Jesus, The. *My Yoke Is Sweet.* North Sydney, NSW, Australia: The Sisters of Saint Joseph of the Most Sacred Heart of Jesus, 1948.

Sisters of Saint Joseph of the Most Sacred Heart of Jesus, The. *Customs and Practices of the Sisters of St. Joseph of the Most Sacred Heart of Jesus.* Sydney: Sisters of Saint Joseph of the Most Sacred Heart of Jesus, 1950.

Sisters of the Brigidine Congregation, The. *The Constitutions of the Sisters of the Brigidine Congregation.* Sydney, NSW, Australia: The Sisters of the Brigidine Congregation, 1956.

Spaull, A. (ed.), *Australian Teachers from Schoolmasters to Militant Professionals.* South Melbourne, Australia: Macmillan. 1977.

Strauss, A. and Corbin, J. *Basics of Qualitative Research.* Newbury Park, California: Sage, 1990.

Strong, D. *Jesuits in Australia.* Richmond, Victoria, Australia: Aurora Books, 1995.

Sturrock, M. *Women of Strength, Women of Gentleness—Brigidine Sisters, Victoria Province.* Melbourne: David Lovell Publishing, 1995.

Sullivan, J. 'Wrestling with managerialism'. In M. Eaton, J. Longmore and A. Naylor (eds.), *Commitment to Diversity: Catholics and Education in a Changing World.* London and New York: Cassell, 2000, pp. 240–259.

Theobald, M. R. 'History of women's education in Australia'. In T. Husen and T. N. Postlethwaite (eds). *The International*

Encyclopaedia of Education. London: Pergamon, 1994, pp. 6731–6735.

———. *Knowing Women: Origins of Women's Education in 19th Century Australia*. Cambridge: Cambridge University Press, 1996.

Tomkins, G. *A Common Countenance: Stability and Change in the Canadian Curriculum*. Scarborough, Ontario, Canada: Prentice-Hall, 1986.

Tormey, A. 'Teaching Orders in Catholic Education in Western Australia 1955–1975: A Historical Study of Changes and Repercussions', unpublished M.Ed. thesis, The University of Western Australia, 1976.

Tranter, J. 'The religious dimension of an Australian religious sisterhood: The Sisters of St. Joseph'. In P. O'Sullivan (ed.), *Religion and Identity*. London: Leicester University Press, 1996.

Trimingham-Jack, C. 'The lay sister in educational history and memory'. Proceedings of the ANZHES Annual Conference, Auckland, New Zealand, 1998.

Turner, N. *Catholics in Australia: A Social History, Vols. 1 & 2*. Victoria, Australia: Collins Dove, 1992.

Victorian Catholic Education Office. *Catholic History Readers* (6 Vols.). Melbourne: Advocate Press, n.d.

Warren, D. 'Messages from the inside: Teachers as clues in history and policy'. *International Journal of Educational Research*. Vol. 13, 1989, pp. 379–390.

Waters, P. M. *The Ursuline Achievement: A Philosophy of Education for Women*. North Carlton, Australia: Colonna, 1994.

West, J. *Daughters of Freedom*. Sutherland, NSW, Australia: Albatross Books, 1997.

White, D. *Education and the State: Federal Involvement in Educational Policy Development*. Victoria, Australia: Deakin University Press, 1987.

Whyte, J. *Church and State in Modern Ireland*. Dublin: Gill and Macmillan, 1971.

Woods, P. *Sociology and the School*. London: Routledge and Kegan Paul, 1983.

Youniss, J. and McLellan, J. A. 'Catholic schools in perspective: Religious identity, achievement, and citizenship'. *Phi Delta Kappan*. October 1999, pp. 105–113.

Index

History of Schools and Schooling

THIS SERIES EXPLORES THE HISTORY OF SCHOOLS AND SCHOOLING in the United States and other countries. Books in this series examine the historical development of schools and educational processes, with special emphasis on issues of educational policy, curriculum and pedagogy, as well as issues relating to race, class, gender, and ethnicity. Special emphasis will be placed on the lessons to be learned from the past for contemporary educational reform and policy. Although the series will publish books related to education in the broadest societal and cultural context, it especially seeks books on the history of specific schools and on the lives of educational leaders and school founders.

For additional information about this series or for the submission of manuscripts, please contact the general editors:

Alan R. Sadovnik
Rutgers University-Newark
Education Dept.
155 Conklin Hall
175 University Avenue
Newark, NJ 07102

Susan F. Semel
The City College of New York, CUNY
138th Street and Convent Avenue
NAC 5/208
New York, NY 10031

To order other books in this series, please contact our Customer Service Department:

800-770-LANG (within the U.S.)
212-647-7706 (outside the U.S.)
212-647-7707 FAX

Or browse online by series at:

www.peterlangusa.com